A Guide to the Wonderful World Around Us

Notes on Nature

By

Brannen Basham

Printed in the United States 2019

Copyright © 2019 by Brannen Basham

Cover and Layout Design: Jill Jacobs

ISBN: 9781093979305

Independently Published
Sprigglys Beescaping
www.sprigglys.com
info@sprigglys.com
@sprigglys_beescaping
[facebook • instagram • youtube]

Printed by Kindle Direct Publishing

Contents

Introduction

CHAPTER 1: THE NATURAL WORLD   12

    Nature is a Loud Place   13
    Sonic Signals   15
    Sunsets   17
    What's in a Mushroom   19
    The Magnetic Field   21
    Snow   23
    Atmosphere   25
    Microscopic Soil Communities   27
    The Moon   31
    Hair   33
    Wind   35
    Slime Mold   37
    The Appalachian Mountains   39

CHAPTER 2: FANTASTIC PLANTS   41

    Caring for Trees   42
    The Underground Society of Roots   45
    The Flashy World of Floral Signage   47
    Picky About Pollinators   49
    Pollen   52
    Seeds   54
    Leaving the Leaves   56
    The Positives of Pest Damage   58
    Festive Parasites   60
    Poison Ivy   62

CHAPTER 3: OUR ANIMAL FRIENDS   64

    Turtles and Tortoises   65
    Avian Aviation   67
    Bivalves: Nature's Water Filters   69
    Spiders   71
    Bats   73
    Frogs and Toads   75
    Earthworms   77
    Opossum Appreciation   79
    Cardinals   81
    Tree Squirrels   83
    Salamanders   85
    Animal Intelligence   87

CHAPTER 4: STRICTLY INSECTS   93
(MOSTLY POLLINATORS)

    North American Pollinators Need Help Too   94
    Carpenter Bees Do More Good Than Harm   97
    Fireflies   99
    Bumble Bee Business   101
    The Wondrous World of Wasps   103
    The Ants Among Us   106
    Attracting Caterpillars to Your Garden   109
    Mason Bees   111
    Insect Mimics   113
    Ladybugs   115
    Bees in Winter   117

CHAPTER 5: HUMAN INNOVATION & IMPACT   119

Paper	120
Natural Dyes	122
The History of Glass	124
A Lick of Salt	126
Bricks	128
Mulch Matters	130
Our Water Supply	132
The Dangers Saturating Our World	134
Insect Decline	138

CHAPTER 6: A LOOK TO THE FUTURE   140

Rising CO_2 Levels Have Far Reaching Effects on Plants	142
Helpful Viruses	145
Plants in Space	147
Solar Fields & Native Plantings	150

EPILOGUE   152

Gardens as Zoos	153

Illustrations

All illustrations were taken from the no attribution Open Source Vectors at Pixabay.com. Thank you to each artist for the beautiful work that brought this book to life.

To my wonderful wife Jill. You are my everything.

Introduction

This guide is a collection of notes on nature covering flora, fauna, and the fantastic wonders of the world around us. There are some special highlights of the Southeastern United States, and even more specifically, of the region where I currently call home in the mountains of Western North Carolina.

I hope you find this guide useful and enjoyable!

Chapter One

THE NATURAL WORLD

Nature is a Loud Place

What truly separates the human species from the rest of the creatures around us? Intricate forms of communication have long been thought to be something that only humans possess. The more we study the different life forms found on Earth, the more this supposition is proved wrong. Whales sing combinations of songs that they have learned from other whales, while some dolphins appear to have distinct 'name' whistles that distinguish themselves from others. Honey bees are known to perform rhythmic dances that communicate the location and abundance of flower sites to other members of their hive. Ants, on the other hand, employ the use of chemical trails to help guide their nest mates to food. Many readers may be familiar with the subtle (and not so subtle) communications that dogs and cats are able to have with their owners. The languages of crows and prairie dogs are so complex that they can have regional dialects. Even bacteria, some of the smallest organisms on the planet, use electrical pulses and chemical signals to organize themselves and cooperate with other bacteria. Everywhere you look, chances are an incredible amount of complex communication is happening without us even realizing it.

Plants have some surprisingly advanced ways of communicating to the world around them both through the air and underground. This can help them prepare for damage caused by pests or grazers. Research has shown that plants in stress are able to disperse clouds of volatile organic compounds that other plants are able to pick up on. Plants that detect these compounds begin to produce chemicals that can help reduce damage by rendering their leaves bitter and less nutritious. In some cases, plants that are under attack release chemicals into the air designed to attract wasps and other beneficial insects who will hopefully chow down on the pests. Some trees are able to actually identify the type of pest by their saliva, in turn releasing compounds specifically engineered to attract that pests' predators. A current hot topic in this field centers on the meaning behind these chemical signals. Some scientists point to a friendly, communicative forest environment with residents that are eager to check up on neighbors and help out when needed. Others believe that plants mostly use these chemical signals in order to communicate with other distant parts of themselves and that plants nearby receive them simply by chance. Whether on purpose or by accident, plants are able to communicate with those around them in other ways as well.

The soil is chock full of many organisms including mycelium, the microscopic fungal threads that surround plant roots and help supply most of the nutrients a plant needs. It turns out that plants actually send signals through these underground networks in order to communicate. Being the witty types that they are, many scientists refer to this as the wood wide web. Research is showing that plants are able to warn each other about incoming threats in this way. They can also share resources with other plants using this network. The oldest trees in a forest are usually connected to a large amount of the plants around them, and they help younger growing plants survive by sending some extra nutrients. Some older trees end up donating all of their energy to the web around them as they die, helping their successors carry on their legacy.

John Donne was correct in far more ways than he realized when he famously penned, "No man is an island entire of itself". For even when we think we are alone, we are constantly receiving communications from the very environment around us.

Sonic Signals

It's no secret that sound is a large part of the way the natural world communicates. Almost everyone is familiar with the various cheeps of birds, the otherworldly calls of cicadas, and the ocean-spanning songs of blue and humpback whales. Sound as we know it is created when an object vibrates and sends sound waves throughout whatever material is around it. Specialized organisms are able to sense these waves and translate them into applicable information. Many organisms use sound as a way to communicate between each other, relying on sound waves to carry their messages far beyond areas that they can see or access. Frogs bellow into the night in search of mates, while crickets listen for friendly chirps through 'ears' on their elbows. Other animals such as bats, dolphins, and some whales have incorporated sound into their hunting techniques, using highly focused sonic blasts to locate prey among their surroundings. Their prey have adapted accordingly, like some moths who rely on radar-absorbing hairs or utilize rapid clicks designed to jam their bat predators.

As life on Earth has gotten progressively louder over the course of its history, almost every frequency has been occupied in the search for open airwaves. Many organisms that intentionally create sound also have specialized organs that are designed to pick up a specific range of sounds most critical to their survival. Our ears are not able to pick up many sounds in the environment that our evolution deemed unnecessary. This distinction is different depending on the organism, however. The same basic restrictions that render a dog whistle inaudible to our ears makes a grasshopper unable to appreciate Van Halen's "Jump".

Advancements in computer and recording technologies have allowed scientists to closely analyze some of the sounds being broadcast in the environment that our ears are unable to pick up. It turns out that a wide variety of seemingly quiet organisms are actually louder than what was originally supposed. Male peacocks use their stately tails to dazzle the eyes and ears of others, as their feathers vibrate and transmit specific frequencies of sound outwards. Some plant roots have been shown to respond to and create minute vibrations, creating local rhythms that might serve as communication. Plants aren't only making noise, however. It appears that a good deal of plants are actually able to sense sonic vibrations and react in different ways. Scientists have found that certain plants are able to follow the sound of running water with their roots, while others listen for the sound of approaching pollinators and increase the nectar content of their flowers within minutes. Studies showed that some plants can even pick up the sounds of caterpillars munching on their leaves and buff up their defenses accordingly. Many insects also use subtle vibrations in order to communicate to each other using sound. An example of this is the 'wake-up call' that honeybees use to energize nestmates; they can also look inside of honeycomb using these vibrations in a way similar to echolocation. Microscopic organisms like bacteria and algae sometimes use sound from their environment as cues for when to grow or move as well.

There are undoubtedly many other ways that organisms use sound to communicate and survive. Unfortunately, it seems that many of these techniques are easily disrupted by noise pollution. Ocean noise from boat traffic seems to be doubling every ten years, forcing blue and humpback whales to change the frequency of their songs and making it harder for them to find mates. On land, noise from cars, planes, and even leaf blowers disrupts the animals that are making or listening for noise. While many of these species can quickly adapt to changes in the sound in their area, try and pay attention to how much you listen to your landscape this year versus how much it's forced to listen to you.

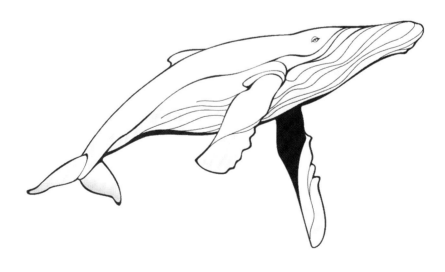

Sunsets

The beauty of a sunset is something rarely matched. As the sun dips below the horizon, the sky is illuminated by golden rays of red, orange, and yellow. Have you ever noticed that these brilliant displays seem to be different depending on where you are? This is not a figment of your imagination—the colors and intensity of a sunset are highly dependent on the air quality and location of the viewing spot. In fact, there are a myriad of factors that go into making a sunset into something truly breathtaking.

The atmosphere itself is the main component of a proper sunset. Sunlight is a white light composed of a full spectrum of colors. As this light comes into contact with our atmosphere, it splinters apart into individual colors. This is known as scattering, and the type and amount of light scattered depends on what's in the air. Oxygen and nitrogen are main contributors to this scattering, and work very well at splintering colors with short wavelengths from sunlight. The blue color of the sky is due to this scattering, as blue and violet are colors with short wavelengths. Scientists believe that the sky is actually a deep violet that our eyes are simply unable to fully process. Sunsets can look so deeply red because as the sun gets closer to the horizon, sunlight is forced to travel through much more atmosphere than normal in order to reach our eyes. By doing so, the sunlight is stripped of most of the shorter wavelength colors and is only left with longer wavelength colors: reds, yellows, and oranges. Sunsets on planets with atmospheres consisting of different gases than Earth's produce radically different colors depending on the composition of the atmosphere. Other ingredients present in the air play a large role in the scattering of sunlight as well.

Microscopic particles in the stratosphere can lead to exceptionally red sunsets. These high flying particles are usually due to volcanoes and forest fires that propel them with help from intense heat. They are able to scatter more blues and violets than a cleaner atmosphere. Scarlet sunsets are also commonly seen near beaches, where the salt content of the air scatters light very effectively. It has been widely circulated that other, low lying types of air pollution like smog can also contribute to stunning sunsets. This is not quite true, however. It seems that most urban air pollution contains particles that are larger and inconsistent in size compared to other air particles. The air pollution commonly found around cities serves to make sunsets brighter but less distinct. In short, with increased air pollution in the lower levels of the atmosphere sunsets can have brighter golden elements but lack the clear colors found elsewhere. On the other end of the spectrum, a sunset viewed from a clear mountaintop will be scattered much less and appear to be more in the white and blue palette.

 Our atmosphere also acts as a lens of sorts, and is able to bend light as it enters. This is the reason that the sun can sometimes appear larger than normal as it sets; as it gets closer to the horizon line, light has to travel through more of our atmosphere, distorting its image. In fact, the sunsets that we gaze upon are an optical illusion. Due to the curvature of the earth's surface and the distortions from our atmosphere, the sun is actually already below the horizon for up to a minute before we perceive it setting with our own eyes. The sunsets that we see are refractions. Similar to how the tip of a stick plunged into water will appear 'disconnected' to the rest of the stick, this has to do with light being warped as it passes through the atmosphere. Regardless of how our eyes perceive sunsets, humans across the world can agree that they are one of the most awe-inspiring sights our planet has to offer.

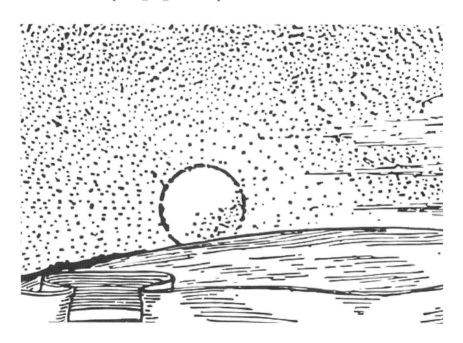

What's in a Mushroom

    To some, the sight of a mushroom is not a memorable event. Scattered throughout our gardens and properties, mushrooms can be found in abundant quantities all over the world. Because of this, the mushroom can be easily overlooked as a mundane regularity. I intend to assure you that the truth is quite the opposite. In fact, mushrooms are components of some of the most successful, interesting, and important organisms on this planet.

    A mushroom is the reproductive part of a much larger fungal organism. Fungi inhabit the soil in incredible numbers, mostly eating dead and decaying material. This alone makes fungi important components in the ecosystem as without them detritus would overwhelm the planet. Luckily for us, fungi thrive in most soils. They are so successful that the largest organism in the world is a fungus in Oregon. Thousands of acres large and thousands of years old, the appropriately named 'humongous fungus' showcases the tenacity and success that fungi have in our environment. One of the reasons for this is the incredible diversity of fungi. These organisms fill roles beyond decomposition, including helping the majority of plants with nutrient and water absorption. The importance of such relationships cannot be overstated: without a healthy population of fungal friends many plants struggle to excel or even survive. Many mushroom producing fungi have close relationships with plants, either working to break down wood or assisting plants in nutrient absorption. Some fungi are even able to kill and eat microscopic prey by setting tiny snare traps.

Different fungi rely on vastly different means of reproduction in order to expand their territory. Many fungi have developed specialized spore producing structures, called mushrooms, in order to reproduce. These structures grow in hiding and wait for the perfect time to emerge. Mushrooms can spend weeks in the soil growing in preparation for their final triumphant burst. When moisture and temperature conditions are just right, mushrooms are able to attain their final glorious form in record speed. Some species fully sprout from the ground in a matter of hours. The mushroom stalk is important at keeping the spore producing top as high off the ground as possible. This allows for spores to be picked up by wind or other means. Mushrooms produce millions of spores and come in a wide variety of shapes and sizes. Some species disperse their spores into the wind, in the hopes that they will come into contact with spores from another mushroom once they land. Others, like the stinkhorn mushroom, utilize foul smells to draw in flies that help transport spores far and wide. There are even mushrooms that glow in the dark to lure in curious insects to disperse their precious spores. With enough time and luck, these spores are eventually able to link up with other spores and create new fungal networks of their own.

In order to reliably find and observe a mushroom in nature, you must first familiarize yourself with the fungus that creates it. Many fungi that create mushrooms have developed an affinity for certain plants that they choose to grow around. If you are searching for a specific mushroom, research their favorite plants to make your hunting more fruitful. Some of the most common tree types that foster mushroom growth in the southeast U.S. are pine, oak, hemlock, and poplar. Without a trained eye, it can be difficult to identify specific mushroom species. Please remember not to pick and eat mushrooms you find unless you are absolutely sure of its type.

If you are interested in observing the growth patterns of mushrooms in a more intimate setting, it can be surprisingly easy to grow them yourself. I recommend you check out the great resources the USDA Agricultural Library has to offer on the subject at https://www.nal.usda.gov/afsic/mushrooms.

The Magnetic Field

There has been increased attention on the Earth's magnetic field in recent years. Scientists have noticed for some time that this protective barrier, which shields the planet from being roasted by cosmic radiation, is less reliable than we might hope. The field itself is generated by iron and other metals circulating deep in the Earth's core. A doctor once described to me that the beating heart is a chaotic, thrashing movement far removed from the peaceful thumps we take it to be. The planet's core is similar. Iron and other metals are constantly moving as the intense heat and pressure at those depths work them like dough. As these metals move differently, the magnetic fields that they emit change accordingly. This can lead to weak spots in the field. Recent studies of the outer layers of our magnetic field have shown that they vibrate like a giant drum every time they are hit with a strong blast of solar wind, helping to disperse harmful radiation while playing out a planetary solo. Scientists have also realized through sample dating that every 250,000 years or so, the polarity of the field flips entirely. We are long overdue for the next polar flip—it's been over 700,000 years since Antarctica was at the North Pole. There is a lot of hype about what exactly a flip in the magnetic field would mean, however. Spurred by the release of some new research on the inner workings of the core itself, I decided it was time to dig deep into what influences our magnetic field and what that means for us surface dwellers.

A large area of the magnetic field is currently weak enough to worry scientists. Known as the South Atlantic Anomaly (SAA), this weak spot lets through enough cosmic radiation to damage satellites that pass through unprepared. The SAA has been under increased scrutiny by the scientific community in an attempt to study the forces behind it. A recent examination of archaeological objects from inside the weak spot has helped show that the core is greatly influenced by the layer of rocks surrounding it, and has been for quite some time. Scientists were able to gather burned clay fragments which included clues to the magnetic field at that time. These showed that the magnetic weak spot has re-occurred throughout history in the same spot. It seems that the SAA is not a new phenomenon, and is at least partly due to the influence of gigantic lumps of metal and rock in the area buried very deep in the planet's center near the core. Scientists believe that these huge structures, called superplumes, change the flow of metals in the core and can lead to molten iron and nickel leaking out into the surrounding rock. This leaking is thought to be a main component to the current weak spots in the magnetic field, and perhaps to the field flipping as well. But what exactly will happen when it does so?

As far as scientists can tell, the polarity of the magnetic field flipping would not be the apocalyptic event some might fear. The flip instead would take perhaps thousands of years. During that time our field will be weaker, which will allow more cosmic rays to enter our atmosphere than before. This should only be a hazard to satellites and other sensitive electronic equipment, which have delicate electrical components that are particularly sensitive. We may also need to wear more sunscreen as more solar radiation is let through. Once the field is flipped, a compass will show what is currently North as South, and all animals that rely on their magnetic sense of direction for migrations will certainly be very confused for a few years. There is no evidence that points to mass extinctions during any of the previous flips. Nature will certainly adapt quickly, leaving us to the task of replacing a lot of burnt out electronics.

Snow

    Let's talk about snow and how to deal with it. I'm sure you are well aware that the beauty of snow is matched only by the pain in the butt it can be. Luckily, armed with the right tools and preparation, you can deal with snow safely in a short amount of time.

    Snow is an important part of our water cycle. Just 2 inches of snow on an acre of land is almost 90,000 pounds of water, possibly more depending on the type of snow. Very wet and heavy snow could weigh twice that much. Snow built up in mountains provides a large amount of the water needed in the growing season. In fact, the U.S. Geological Survey (USGS) estimates that some western states rely on melting snow for as much as 75% of their water. Ancient Romans were known to routinely collect snow from atop Mt. Etna in order to create the precursor to gelato, while hundreds of years before that Incas in Chile used snow to preserve mummies in mountain caves. All this from a collection of minute ice crystals formed high in our atmosphere.

    Snow can serve to insulate plants during harsh winter months, and in really cold areas like Alaska it's actually used to help insulate houses. This is because snow is nearly 90% air. Plants protected by a layer of snow are able to better withstand rapid temperature changes during the winter. Be aware that while leaving snow on your plants can help them survive extreme temperatures, it can also harbor pests. If left to their own devices in bad winters, small rodents can tunnel through snow to nibble at your plants. Although leaving some snow around plants can be helpful, make sure to keep it from being in direct contact with the bark and base of trees and shrubs for prolonged periods. Many times the roots of a plant are what needs the most insulation rather than the trunk. Also keep an eye out for overburdened tree limbs during the winter months. Even strong limbs can become dangerously heavy especially after ice storms. This can lead to large chunks of snow and ice or even whole branches coming loose and falling.

 Snow removal is a game of preparation and proactiveness. In long and heavy storms, shovel frequently to keep the snow from becoming too oppressive to remove. No matter how you decide to deal with snow, you will have to also deal with ice. One option is to apply an ice melting substance in spots that you expect to become slippery immediately before the storm if possible. While commercial ice melts are relatively quick and easy to apply, most can actually cause significant damage to asphalt, plants, and/or the surrounding soil. Calcium magnesium acetate (CMA) is an eco-friendly ice melt that I have seen work very well. Re-apply during and immediately after the storm to ensure that ice never has a chance to form in these areas. Make sure to read directions and only use as much ice melt as necessary to avoid runoff. Some current research is showing that road concrete mixed with certain materials such as paraffin wax can actually melt snow and ice on its own! Hopefully one day shoveling will be a thing of the past.

 I also like to use sand liberally on my property, sprinkled in any spot that may be or may become slippery. Keep in mind that while sand provides a good deal of traction it does not actively melt ice. This means that sand might have to be reapplied to icy spots if it becomes iced over during the night. By taking steps to limit snow and ice buildup before and during a storm you can save yourself a good deal of time and energy. To avoid any additional wintry battles, make sure to leave your shoes outside.

Atmosphere

The movements of underwater creatures can sometimes appear to be more labored than those of landlubbers. This is due to the fact that the water they are moving through is generally a thousand times denser than air. However we're constantly engulfed by a sea of sorts as well—our atmosphere. Except during especially humid summer afternoons, it can be easy to forget that we are immersed in a bubble of gases. The incredible frailty of this situation deserves a moment of reflection. The collection of gases that sustain all life on Earth is held in place by the gravitational pull of our planet, a planet that spins through our solar system at 67,000 miles per hour while being bombarded by blasts of solar radiation. Yet with help from our planet's magnetic fields, which help shield it from solar winds, most of our atmosphere manages to cling on as we hurtle through space. This is pretty good for us. The air surrounding Earth has far reaching impacts into every aspect of life, but how did it get there?

The air around our planet has no clearly defined edge, however most scientists refer to a line 62 miles high off the surface as where outer space begins. Earth's air weighs in at around 5,000,000,000,000,000 tons. Our atmosphere first came into being during the creation of our planet, as lightweight gases were drawn in by the gravity of primitive Earth while the molten core spewed clouds of various gases. These gases slowly built up and their weight began to press down onto the surface. This atmospheric pressure is key in keeping liquid water on the surface of Earth, as once atmospheric pressure drops too low water quickly boils away. Our barren neighbor Mars is a good example of this, as we have found evidence that water once flowed over its red surface. At some point Mars seems to have lost its atmosphere, and along with it any liquid surface water it might have had.

The composition of the Earth's atmosphere has changed over time due to the geological processes and organisms occurring at different periods. For example, the atmosphere in the Jurassic period had an estimated 5 times the amount of CO_2 compared to ours due largely to erupting volcanoes. This was slowly whittled away and turned into different gases by various causes and organisms. At a certain point in the

Earth's history so much oxygen was saturating the air that it led to mass extinctions of the dominant life forms at that time. The concentration of different elements in the atmosphere has far reaching effects on the organisms living on the planet, since each organism requires a unique cocktail of elements in order to survive and thrive. The relationship goes both ways, however, as living creatures have also played a large role in the composition of our atmosphere. Plants are a major influence on our current atmosphere as they consume carbon dioxide and pump oxygen into the air. This oxygen leads to rapid growth in animal populations, which then exude other gases into the atmosphere. Oxygen currently makes up about 21% of the air we breathe. The combination of geological processes and organisms has created the unique mix of gases all around us, however it will constantly change as new organisms arise and geology winds its course.

Besides containing the oxygen and other elements necessary to our existence, Earth's atmosphere ensures our survival by reducing temperature extremes during the night and day, shielding us from harmful solar radiation, and keeping the planet warm enough to support life. Luckily the hole in the protective ozone layer, which helps shield the surface from solar radiation, is showing signs of repairing itself. This is largely due to the reduced use of chlorofluorocarbons (CFCs), the chemicals responsible for a buildup of ozone-destroying chlorine in the atmosphere. While the ozone layer seems to be stabilizing, it's still a good idea to consider ways that you can prevent undesirables from entering the air. After all, we're practically swimming in it.

Microscopic Soil Communities

When thinking about the most valuable natural resources, the first things that come to mind are usually oil, gemstones, precious metals, and other similar commodities. You may be surprised to hear that one of the most important and truly priceless natural resources is soil. Soil is thought to have started forming long ago as tiny organisms moved from the oceans onto land. Algae, bacteria, and other microscopic organisms built colonies on rocky shorelines and as they died other organisms grew on top of them. As these layers started to build up, opportunistic lichen spread further onto the rocky surface of early Earth. Rock dwelling lichen release weak acids and played an invaluable role in dissolving the surface of the planet into nutrient-rich soil. This process slowly led to the layers of soil we know today. Modern soil is filled with many of the nutrients required to sustain life. It even sequesters a huge amount of carbon which helps in the fight against rapid global warming.

Microscopic organisms throughout history have captured carbon from the air and stored it in the soil in the form of a recently discovered protein called glomalin. A huge variety of microorganisms have taken up residence inside the soil where they perform their work unseen. Each handful of soil likely contains billions of organisms that work in tandem. It seems that around 70% of all bacteria and other microorganisms live underground, quite literally doing the dirty work required to keep the natural world functioning. Scientists are constantly finding strange and mysterious creatures beneath the surface of our soils. The combination of nutrient rich soil and a diverse community of organisms that work to transform those nutrients into usable forms is one of the key factors behind most of the life on Earth, and living soil is something that we have yet to find on other planets.

One of the primary drivers behind healthy soil is bacteria. There are a wide variety of soil bacteria that perform tasks related to breaking down material. While they decompose matter, bacteria help supply the nutrients necessary for most plant and animal life. Some bacteria are even able to consume hazardous pollutants such as pesticides. The nutrient content of soil is heavily influenced by the type and number of bacteria living inside it. Soil without bacteria is eventually useless once the nutrients inside are all used up. Healthy ecosystems rely on a healthy balance of bacteria to revitalize the dirt. For example, the roots of many legumes encourage the growth of beneficial bacteria which transform nitrogen from the air into a plant-friendly form. The host plants help feed the bacteria in exchange for nitrogen. Some other types of bacteria are able to infect and damage plants. These usually prefer anaerobic and compact soils, so make sure to keep your soil well drained in problem areas.

Bacteria are not only limited to the soil and are found in large amounts basically everywhere on the planet. Interestingly some of these bacteria emit ultraviolet light through certain compounds in their cells. Even though we are unable to see these ultraviolet displays, insects such as aphids have been found to avoid concentrations of deadly bacteria based on sight alone. Certain common soil bacteria have also been directly linked with reduced stress and anxiety when ingested by humans. If you're ever feeling blue in the garden, maybe try and stick that green thumb in your mouth. Studies have shown that bacterial communities are incredibly diverse—the types of bacteria found on your shoes are very different than the ones found on your cell phone. It is still largely unknown how these many organisms impact our health, however the amount of beneficial bacteria is far more than the dangerous ones. While it may seem that the world is constantly overrun by microscopic bacteria, their populations in the soil are largely kept in check by nematodes, another important microscopic soil dweller.

Nematodes do not break down matter, but instead feed on live prey. Most of these tiny worm-like animals feed on bacteria, fungi, and other tiny organisms. Some nematodes are used to combat invasive insect pests instead of chemical applications. A small amount of nematodes feed on plant roots or bark and can damage plants or spread disease through their feeding—nematodes can be difficult to diagnose, however. If you have a problem area with damage or disease without any other obvious reason why, try planting some marigolds between your plantings. These have been known to keep damaging nematodes at bay. Having generally healthy soil also helps prevent large buildups of nematodes as certain fungi trap and eat any wandering 'tode that comes nearby.

Microscopic fungi fill diverse roles in soil. Some types of fungi have evolved to work alongside plants in symbiotic relationships. These partnerships usually involve the fungus surrounding a plant's roots and helping that plant with nutrient and moisture absorption in exchange for nutrients from the host. Fungi are also a food source for many other organisms as they help to break down material. Many fungi have above ground growths as well such as mushrooms. These are used for food and shelter by a wide variety of wildlife. Larger creatures also live in the soil such as bumble bees, thousands of solitary bee and wasp species, ants, yellow jackets, and worms, not to mention the various mammals and amphibians that tunnel happily in the upper layers of the soilosphere. Many of these animals mix the soil, helping to spread the important work that our many microscopic dirt dwellers are constantly performing. The next time you see soil, take a moment to appreciate the vast and powerful ecosystems contained in even the smallest sample.

The Moon

Over 4 billion years ago, a young Earth collided with another large object thought to be around the size of Mars. Luckily it was mostly a glancing blow, however the planetary bump resulted in huge chunks of both Earth and the other object coming loose and floating in orbit nearby. Over millions of years these formed into our single moon. The moon has been constantly pelted by asteroids and other cosmic bullies just as the Earth has. Unlike the Earth, due to the lack of an atmosphere, our moon bears the scars from these attacks for a very long time. Many of the dark spots that we see on the surface are in fact huge impact craters that were filled with lava long after their creation. These dried lava flows are so immense that they can cause gravitational anomalies that disrupt orbiting spacecraft. Our moon is unusually large and dense compared to other known moons, and this contributes to the profound changes that it has on the Earth's climates and oceans.

Throughout the billions of years that the Earth and our moon have been locked together by gravity, our movements have changed significantly. It is believed that the moon originally moved four times faster and was much closer to the Earth than it is currently. This had profound impacts on the global tides, which follow the moon's movements in their rising and falling. The Earth's gravitational pull helped slow the moon's pace to the current synchronous rotation, which is around 29 days to both rotate itself and orbit the Earth. This means that we always see the same side of the moon. The gravity from the moon has also impacted the Earth's movements as well, leading to slower spinning and less global wobbling. In short, the moon allows for more reliable seasons and winds that are less intense than seen elsewhere in the solar system. Huge gravitational forces such as the ones in play between the Earth and our moon can trap other objects in specific areas, and scientists believe they recently discovered proof of multiple 'ghost moons' made up of dust clouds circling the planet. While these clouds lack the ability to be as bright as the moon, in truth the lunar surface is not the pearly white it can appear. Astronauts and scientists have compared the color of the moon to asphalt, which looks bright mainly due to reflective dust and the darkness of the space behind it.

Excitement for Martian exploration is causing many nations to leave our moon in the shadows in terms of further on-the-ground missions. Recent data is showing that the moon may have more to offer than previously thought, however. It is believed that as comets and other celestial objects impact the moon and Earth, they bring with them traces of water among other things. While most water on the lunar surface is quickly boiled away in sunlight due to the extremely thin atmosphere, scientists predict that over 5,000 square miles of the lunar surface are constantly dark. These shadowy nooks and crannies, mostly near the poles and at the bottom of craters, were found to have the lowest temperatures ever recorded by a spacecraft at around negative 400 degrees Fahrenheit. Multiple projects over the years have used reflective analysis and other measures to determine that there is probably a surprising amount of frozen water sheltered in the dark regions of the moon. Small amounts of water are also believed to be sheltered under the layers of lunar dust found covering the moon. This dust is made of rocks and volcanic glass and reportedly carries a slight gunpowder odor. Lunar water stores are estimated to be about as rich as those of the driest deserts on Earth, however perhaps they could be enough to help support a human colony in the future. China has picked up the slack in lunar exploration, and they have recently sent a rover to the far side of the moon for the first time. Hopefully their expedition will find more interesting information about the makeup and creation of our nearest cosmic neighbor.

Hair

When it's cold outside, a coat is usually one of the first things to reach for when trying to stay warm. Humans are not alone in this respect. In the wintertime, mammals of all shapes and sizes rely on a thick coat of densely packed hairs, also known as fur, in order to survive the cold. This multilayered bulwark, built of several types of hair each with a special purpose, serves to keep water at bay while retaining warm air near the skin. These hairs are able to manipulate the flow of air and temperature to a remarkable degree. The incredible effectiveness of fur as an insulator has been used as inspiration for human clothing and building materials for centuries, but it has never been matched. Research into the unique ways that fur scatters and collects infrared radiation is beginning to shed some light into how exactly an animal like a polar bear can survive temperatures of -40 degrees Fahrenheit with only two inches of fur. While we may hopefully one day unlock the secrets to fur's amazing warming capabilities, animals in every climate have found ways to use hair to their own benefit.

Hair can almost be thought of as evolution's duct tape—it can be used to solve a seemingly endless variety of problems. Different types of animals utilize hair in a variety of unique ways. Insects rely on hairs for gripping surfaces, collecting pollen, and self-cleaning. Some caterpillars use dense, prickly patches of venomous hair as defense against predators. There is even a type of crab that uses lush arm hairs to grow colonies of bacteria for food. While these are all very interesting, over time mammals have become the world's prime hair-havers. Hair helps mammals survive in a multitude of ecosystems and environments, propelling them to the top of many food chains.

Most mammals utilize multiple types of hair in order to help them survive. A cat, for instance, has a layered coat of fur but also sensory hairs—called whiskers—that help give an early sign of quick movement in the immediate area. Highly sensitive whiskers help give cats incredibly fast reactions to anything nearby, however they are not unique in the mammal kingdom. Our eyelashes are very similar to whiskers and tend to induce an involuntary blink when brushed against. Hedgehogs use huge, reinforced hairs to prick away any unwanted attention while cotton top tamarin monkeys use flamboyant hairstyles to attract others. In stark contrast to animals who rely on hair to stay warm, some animals are able to utilize hair to stay cool instead. Elephants use sparse, wiry hairs to aid in venting heat. The coats on dogs and monkeys work wonders at keeping UV rays off of the skin, and while they can be quite dense most allow for decent heat loss. Many animals are able to make their hairs stand up to increase their insulating abilities. A good example of this mechanism can be seen on humans in a cold breeze, as the muscles causing goose bumps would have also raised the hairs on our body if we still had them. Interestingly, humans are one of the only mammals that have undergone significant hair loss over time as a species.

The reasons that humans are no longer as hairy as our simian ancestors are largely unknown and hotly debated. Prevailing theories revolve around the need for humans to shed most of our hair as our cramped social societies led to pests like fleas and lice. As we lost more hair, humans also began to rely more heavily on sweating in order to keep cool. This helped us stay active during the hottest parts of the day, when many other creatures are forced to find shelter in the cool of shade. Some scientists believe that this was one of the main reasons early humans became so successful. No matter the shape, length, or color, appreciate your locks; hair has helped countless animals survive the elements.

Wind

As the Earth rotates through space and orbits the sun, different parts of the globe are heated by sunlight as they turn to face the day. During the daytime, the land and air exposed to solar heat warm up. When air is heated its molecules spread out and begin moving upwards—think of a bucket of water being scooped skyward from the ocean. This movement leaves a relatively low-pressure area behind, which is then flooded with the surrounding air much like water rushing in to fill the space left behind by a bucket of scooped water. The haphazard rush of air into the space left behind by warm rising air is what we know as wind. While in some parts of the world the power and direction of wind is relatively reliable, landscape differences such as mountains and valleys can cause winds to take wild and unpredictable turns. The rotation of the earth also alters the flow of the winds, causing them to veer either right or left depending on the hemisphere. Even though winds are constantly changing due to differences in heating day by day, the process of air moving to fill up spaces left behind by rising air has created one of the most impactful natural forces on our planet.

Winds have drastically changed the surface of the planet over millions of years. Many of the deserts on Earth were formed when plant life died out in the area. One of the most important roles plants play is holding soil in place; once there are no plants, winds quickly rid the area of everything but rocks and sand. By throwing small particles like sand and pebbles onto larger rocks, wind is also able to wear down even the highest mountains. This is due in part to the high speeds winds can reach. Even at ground level, where wind speeds are generally the lowest, wind speeds have been recorded at over 250 mph where large masses of air at different temperatures come together. Earth isn't the only planet to experience winds. In fact, our weather seems to be pretty tame even in our own solar system. By throwing a probe into the atmosphere of nearby planets and observing how they fall, scientists have determined that the planets beyond Mars are gusty on an immense scale. Neptune, for example, is thought to experience winds of almost 900 mph. Even though the wind on our planet pales in comparison, if we were able to harness the energies of even a small portion of the winds on Earth we could solve energy demands for the foreseeable future.

While wind power has been in heavy development since the 1970s, recent breakthroughs have led to some interesting new design ideas for generating power. One of the major drawbacks of most wind projects is their immense size. In order to generate sufficient power at ground level, huge towers must usually be constructed to hold the immense turbines of commercial operations. These towers disrupt natural ecosystems and can even harm bats and birds unlucky enough to wander close. Such problems could be a thing of the past as scientists are testing new kite-like wind turbines that are able to remain aloft in the air without the need for bulky towers, while taking advantage of the more powerful winds found at higher altitudes. The maritime shipping industry is also turning to wind power to once again help deliver their goods—this time, with immense kites designed to help pull heavy loads. With new wind-based technologies emerging almost daily, perhaps we will soon be able to more effectively utilize this powerful and abundant resource with minimal impact on the natural world.

Slime Molds

After a few days of summer rain, a common sight among lawns and mulched garden beds is a brightly-colored mass of what looks like fungus or algae. This creature, ranging from neon yellow to white, is usually called dog vomit fungus due to its charming appearance. Don't be fooled, however. These are actually what's known as slime molds, and not only are they of no harm to your plants, family, or pets, but they actually hunt microscopic organisms in the garden that could potentially harm your plantings. Watch your step as we learn a bit about how slime molds accomplish this by utilizing some unique and astonishing feats.

Originally grouped with fungi, the over 900 known species of slime molds are now referred to as protists. This basically means that they cannot be categorized as plant, fungus, or animal. Scientists are still trying to work out where they fit in beyond that. Most slime molds are huge congregations of single-celled organisms. These tiny organisms are able to survive alone in times of plentiful food, however they can also join together in order to travel larger distances in search of a meal. In some cases, the organisms actually fuse together to form a single giant cell with multiple nuclei, kind of like thousands of individuals taking shelter inside of a mobile bubble. Other types of slime molds release chemical signals to draw in others and make swarms of individual cells that work in tandem but don't physically fuse together. In both cases, slime molds are able to do some fascinating things in their mobile congregations, known as their plasmodial form.

Warm, humid nights in the summer are the perfect time for slime molds to come together and take to their plasmodial shapes. As they do so, these organisms are able to quickly move (for a slime) through their environment in search of prey. They can detect the smell of tasty yeasts, fungi, and bacteria, and as they move slime molds engulf their victims to be digested inside of the moving community. As conditions become unfavorable for them, they typically dry up and release spores, repeating the process until moisture returns. Scientists have been fascinated by the abilities of slime molds for quite some time. As they explore an area, slime molds leave behind trails that help keep them from visiting the same place twice. Studies on these organisms show that although they do not have brains, they are able to restructure themselves to form extremely efficient connections between food sources. Slime molds are so quick and effective at establishing these connections that engineers have used them as inspiration for building transportation systems of our own. Slime molds are also apparently able to assess the nutritional quality of the food that they come into contact with and prefer to eat high quality food over junk food, a trait in which they far surpass the writer. Studies have even shown that in some cases these organisms are able to tell time and can anticipate periodic events. Not bad for something that at first glance makes many run for the pooper scooper.

Slime molds do not last in their plasmodial form for long, as the dry heat of day is usually enough to reduce them to dust quickly. They will usually only be around for a few days, especially if the weather dries out. If the slime molds in and around your property become unsightly, stirring them into your mulch with a rake or spraying them off with a strong jet of water is usually sufficient. Try to give them time to produce spores and complete their life cycle, however, because although these organisms can be unsightly they are also helping to keep the various yeasts, bacteria, and fungi on your property in check.

The Appalachian Mountains

In Western North Carolina, mountains are a part of everyday life. While the mountains here are awe-inspiring on a daily basis, many times the historical, industrial, or geological importance of the Appalachian Mountains are easily overlooked or forgotten.

The Appalachian Mountains separate the east coast from the Midwest, and were first formed around 300 million years ago when the modern-day continents of Africa and North America slammed together. Like an immense car crash, this collision caused the crumpling and rising of the earth's crust in the area. In the following millions of years these mountains remained as the continents broke apart and formed the land masses we are familiar with today. The Appalachian Mountains are some of the oldest in the world and were once as tall as the Alps, however they have been slowly whittled down by erosion. Throughout their history, they have acted in weather manipulation, been a source of refuge to many different species, and they have gifted us with a wide variety of natural resources.

The uniquely lush Appalachian Mountain environment is due in large part to the mountains themselves. As winds make their journey around the globe, mountains act as ramps that drive them up into colder altitudes. In general, for every 1,000 feet in altitude the temperature drops up to five degrees. This causes moisture in the air to condense into clouds and precipitation. The mountains effectively wring the moisture out of the winds. Since the Appalachian Mountains have been in place for millions of years, they have been able to make the surrounding landscape wetter and in consequence more amenable to a wide variety of life for a very long time. A good deal of the southern Appalachian range is actually considered a temperate rainforest, making it the only one on the east coast of North America. This moisture has also worn down the Appalachians, allowing for the minerals within to be more easily discovered by humans. The Appalachians are relatively rich in mineral diversity; prospectors have been known to find rubies, sapphires, emeralds, garnets, and quartz as well as gold, lead, copper, and zinc hidden in the rocks and streambeds that dot the mountainsides. Many of the Appalachian Mountains have also been tapped for coal, oil, and natural gas deposits.

The southern Appalachians have been home to a large number of unique native animals. It is believed that there were even several types of smaller tyrannosaurs that once used the ancient mountains as their exclusive hunting ground. According to the Blue Ridge National Heritage Area, the mountains of North Carolina are home to more species of plants than any other area of similar size in North America. As urbanization has slowly spread through the country, the mountains have served as a last refuge for many imperiled species such as bear, wolves, panthers, mink, and otter. The mountains also harbor populations of salamanders, speckled trout, and hemlocks that are struggling elsewhere.

Unfortunately, the Appalachians have been heavily affected by human history as well. Many of these mountain landscapes are in the process of recovering from damage incurred through extensive logging and coal mining in the early 1900s. Chestnut trees, once a major part of the Appalachian landscape, were also effectively wiped out in the early 1900s due to a fungal disease. The battle continues: many of our native forest species are currently under attack by invasive pests and diseases, such as the hemlock woolly adelgid and beech bark disease. Fortunately, the Appalachian Mountains' ability to support a wide variety of life might give scientists just the time they need to figure out at least some of the solutions to these problems.

Chapter Two

FANTASTIC PLANTS

Caring for Trees

There are many reasons to care about the trees around you. Trees are some of the oldest and most important organisms on this planet. There is no specific taxonomic group for trees, instead they are classified as perennial plants that have their branches and leaves held up by a long woody stem, otherwise known as a trunk. Trees fed the dinosaurs and paved the way for our emergence in the world. In fact, trees have emitted so much oxygen over the years that they changed the composition of our atmosphere. The haze and color surrounding the Blue Ridge Mountains is a good example of just how much trees can exhale—the mountains owe much of their signature hue to the fact that they are so heavily forested. Trees possess an incredible amount of variety. There are trees that engage in chemical warfare such as the sassafras and black walnut, warding off pests, diseases, and other plants by poisoning the soil they live in. Other trees incorporate heavy metals into their stems and leaves to help ward off damaging insects. The tallest trees are taller than a 25-story building while the shortest are only inches high. There are even trees in South America that can move a few centimeters a day.

If this wasn't impressive enough, studies have shown that trees and other plants actually communicate with each other through chemical signaling. It seems that plants use arrangements of calcium ions in their cells to create electrical pulses. At the first sign of damage in a leaf, these pulses are sent throughout the plant. In only a few minutes the entire plant is keen on the attack and is able to respond. Some trees release potent chemicals into their leaves to prevent further damage while others disperse chemical clouds into the air that can travel long distances to warn other trees of a coming invasion. This helps give them an early warning sign for any danger heading their way. While these are all fascinating, the truth is that scientists have only scratched the surface of the complicated networks behind plant communication. For all we know, the trees in our backyards could be discussing the last season of *Stranger Things* over our very shoulders.

Large, well established trees require very little care to thrive. Many trees are able to survive grievous wounds and crippling droughts all on their own, especially trees growing in their native region. Make sure to stay well away from the base of trees with any heavy equipment, however. Even a riding lawn mower is heavy enough to compact the ground around tree roots, squeezing out any water or air in the soil and making it harder for water and nutrients to percolate down to the tree. Young and newly planted trees will benefit greatly from a little additional help as well. During the first 3 years of a newly planted tree's life it is important that they receive enough water to survive. As long as the tree gets a few inches of water several times a week, it will be able to establish the stronger roots needed to sustain a larger plant. The winter can be a tough time for young trees due to freezing temperatures, pest damage, and harsh winds. There are a few simple things you can do to give your trees the best winter possible. Smaller and newly planted trees are especially susceptible to damage from freezing temperatures and pests. Place some mulch around the base of your trees if needed; 1 to 2 inches will be enough to help insulate roots from freezing temperatures. Fallen leaves also work as a mulch if you have a good supply. Make sure you do not pile mulch around the base of the tree, as this could cause excessive moisture to build up on the trunk which is usually a bad thing.

Trees with a small diameter, especially those near the edges of clearings, are very attractive to deer. Rowdy bucks mark their territory over the fall and winter seasons by rubbing trees with their antlers and removing large portions of branches and bark. This can be devastating to a tree, as it destroys the cambium layer containing the system that brings nutrients from root to leaf. Wrapping the bottom 4 to 5 feet of small trees with a heavy wrapping or heavy-duty deer fence can help ward off rubbing. In areas with large deer populations, almost any young tree will need to be protected. Deer are apparently confused by multiple layers of fencing. For problem areas, a double layer of fences a few inches apart can work well at keeping deer at bay. Deer also dislike stepping through piles of sticks—Native Americans were known to surround young trees with several rings of stick piles in order to fend them off.

If you have your own property, take a walk around and keep a keen eye out for any dead or weird looking limbs in your trees. Pay special attention to trees around houses or roads. Dead or wonky limbs will be the first to go in a winter storm. Consider having them removed in the fall before they become a real hazard later on. Keep in mind that it is always beneficial to leave fallen or cut limbs on your property when possible. If a closely manicured yard is your style, try to tuck these limbs away in an unseen area of your landscape. Even a small amount of fallen limbs can offer habitat for a wide range of wildlife. The fall and winter are ideal times for pruning your trees, so as the temperature drops perhaps start thinking about tidying up a few of those unruly masses your neighbors keep dropping hints about.

The Underground Society of Roots

Even during a cold and desolate winter, beneath the soil plant roots are in an active state of growth and preparation. These roots are the hidden workhorses of plants, providing structural support, water, and nutrients that are critical to survival. Roots of many plants take advantage of the insulation provided by the soil above them and continue to grow as long as the ground is not frozen. This leads to roots being able to accomplish some amazing feats. In general, looking at a plant is similar to gazing upon an iceberg—a large majority of a plant's structure exists out of sight, underground. Most roots extend far beyond the branch tips of the above-ground plant, and underneath a forest floor is an intricate collection of intermingling roots. The roots of plants in the same species commonly join together where they meet. In fact, one of the largest organisms in the world is a huge collection of aspen trees in Utah that all share the same gargantuan root system. Known as Pando, the organism occupies over 100 acres. This is due in large part to the fact that roots are remarkably adaptable and resilient, able to survive extreme conditions and rejuvenate their above ground plant structures year after year.

In many perennial plants, smaller roots are killed off as the ground freezes, leaving a framework of larger, woody roots that regenerate the small delicate feeder roots yearly. These hardier roots are able to enter a dormant state as it freezes, and quickly spring back into action as soon as it thaws. Most roots tend to lie in the top layers of soil since that is where the most nutrients are found. These are some of the only rules that roots follow, however. In their search for oxygen, water, and nutrients, roots will take advantage of the easiest path to supply whatever the plant needs. As such, roots are known as advantageous and will grow in a variety of ways depending on the needs of the plant. If it is necessary to penetrate deep into the ground to find water, plants will form large tap roots capable of descending to great depths. The deepest of these tap roots yet discovered reached almost 400 feet! Some plants such as the potato utilize specialized roots to store nutrients. Trees, on the other hand, grow immense networks of shallow, creeping roots that help to support their huge weight while also supplying nutrients and water.

The soil surrounding a plant's roots is just as active as the leaves and branches. An enormous variety of organisms tunnel and chew through the soil in search of underground food and housing. By doing so, they help to decompress and aerate the soil, making it easier for the nutrients found inside water and air to penetrate deep into the soil where they can be available for roots to absorb. Roots don't necessarily do this by themselves, however. Many plants' roots have developed symbiotic relationships with certain types of fungi. These helpful root fungi, called mycorrhizae, are nutrient super-highways. Over 75% of plants rely on help from root fungi. Many of these fungi aid in nutrient transportation, effectively increasing the surface area that roots have and improving their efficiency. Other root types harbor populations of bacteria that help transform nitrogen into a usable form in exchange for shelter and nutrients from the host plant. There has even been research pointing to root fungi linking plants together, allowing them to share resources. Some of these fungal networks also help plant roots by killing microscopic root eaters like nematodes and bacteria.

The soil is home to a bustling world where roots act as prime players. Roots in their many forms pave the way for above ground ecosystems by providing plants with the support, water, and nutrients that they need.

The Flashy World of Floral Signage

While many of us take pleasure in being around blooming plants because of their beauty, a closer look reveals the true nature of flowers. What might at first glance appear to be a peaceful wildflower meadow is actually the site of frenzied activity. For many creatures on Earth, a collection of flowers is more akin to Las Vegas during rush hour than it is to the relaxing image we take it to be. Many plants have developed flowers with advanced combinations of sights, smells, and other cues that help them attract the visitors they want while excluding unwanted guests. In fact, these plants are actively competing against each other in order to attract the most desirable pollinators. We are still constantly learning about the different ways that plants use flowers to attract visitors, however what we already know may change the way you look at flowers forever.

To put it bluntly, plants have been using flowers to manipulate animals for millions of years. Flowering plants mostly require that their pollen be transported from plant to plant by another organism in order to produce the most fertile seed. So, they lure in animals (usually insects) with nectar, in hopes that they will come into contact with sticky pollen and visit flowers on other plants of the same species. In this process, the unwitting animal exchanges pollen between the two plants and ensures proper fertilization. Magnolia trees are a good example of where floral attraction first started some 200 million years ago. Magnolia flowers today still look similar to how the first flowers did. The prime pollinators at that time were beetles: slow, clumsy flyers that needed a highly visible and easily accessible landing pad. Magnolia flowers form the perfect bullseye for beetles to locate and are also easy to land on. As plants and animals continued to evolve alongside each other, flowers became much more complicated in order to accomplish specific tasks.

Many modern-day flowers look very different to us than they do to pollinators. For example, a good deal of flowers possess markings visible in the ultraviolet spectrum. These markings are invisible to the human eye yet assist in guiding pollinators to the nectar they are looking for. This allows for the most efficient pollination visits. Some flowers even change their appearance after pollination, giving curious animals in the area the heads-up that they should move on. The scents that flowers give off are also complex signals that serve to attract specific pollinators. Many flowers don't only emit scents from one location, instead relying on patterns of scent organs located throughout the bloom. Bumble bees have been found to be able to read these scent patterns and associate them with their favorite flowers. Attractive floral adaptations give plants the ability to 'pick and choose' who visits their blooms, choosing those species which most effectively pollinate that specific plant. Some plants, like the native bottle gentian, even go so far as to have flowers that allow access to only a select few species.

Recent studies have started to show that flowers use some other extreme measures to attract pollinators. It's been found that flowers have unique electrical fields due to tiny structures on their petals. Pollinators, bees in particular, are able to sense these electrical fields and it is believed they can glean some pretty amazing information such as the type of flower and even if there has been a recent visitor. These electrical fields also help pollen stick to pollinators. Some night blooming flowers have hot spots that serve to help guide pollinators as well. This can really help in the dark!

Flowering plants go all-out in order to advertise their willingness for visitors. Just like the glittering boulevards of Vegas, however, there is a deeper reason behind all of the glamour—the house always wins.

Picky About Pollinators

For the vast majority of plants, pollination is critical to the health of current and future generations. Pollination among plants allows for the creation of seeds, larger fruit, and increases genetic diversity, leading to a greater resistance to environmental stressors. In order to achieve the most efficient pollination possible, some plants have developed close relationships with specific animals. Agave plants produce flowers on tall stalks to lure in bats while fig trees rely on highly specialized wasps for pollination. The native bottle gentian, preferring bumble and carpenter bees over all others, possesses a flower with closed petals that most insects simply can't open. Only those strong enough to pry open the petals are allowed the honor of pollinating such a regal bloom. By choosing to support certain pollinators over others, these plants are able to fine tune their flower shape and bloom time in order to more easily attract the most efficient pollinators. Some plants, like rhododendrons, azaleas, and mountain laurels, take their pollinator pickiness to a whole new level. These plants produce powerful neurotoxins which actually harm or kill unwelcome diners.

Rhododendrons seem to produce more than 25 types of these toxins, called grayanotoxins. The plants distribute these throughout their leaves in order to help ward off pests. It appears that many of these toxins work in tandem with each other to increase the effectiveness of the chemical defense. Each plant has a specific blend of toxins, which can change due to stimuli from the outside environment. Some plants even alter their chemical defenses depending on how much light they receive in order to make the deadliest cache. A grazer with no experience in rhododendron meals would have a bad time after eating these laced leaves. Grayanotoxins are also found in the nectar of rhododendrons and have been documented killing honey bees and other unwanted floral visitors. European honey bees are not completely excluded from rhododendron dining, however. While honey bees are rarely able to feed on North American native rhododendrons, they have been known to actively collect and store nectar from rhododendrons native to the Mediterranean, which is where honey bees originated from. In heavy enough quantities, this honey can cause nausea and disorientation. There are several stories throughout ancient history of this honey being used to varying degrees, including a Roman army who were tricked into eating their full, and who were then ambushed while under its effects. The poisonous nature of North American rhododendron nectar to honey bees is simply a product of the fact that honey bees did not evolve alongside these plants.

Like other specialized plants, rhododendrons have designed their blooms to attract their favorite pollinators. Saturating their nectar with toxins adds another layer to the ways in which these plants seek to attract specific pollinators. Certain native bees like bumble bees and the azalea miner bee are immune to the toxins found in North American rhododendrons, and happily feed on their nectar. These bees are far more effective at pollinating native rhododendrons than honey bees and other pollinators, and so it makes sense that the plants would prefer their visits. The grayanotoxins present in rhododendron nectar raise another question. If their preferred pollinators disappeared, would the rhododendron unwittingly poison any alternative pollinator who tried to help as it declined as a species?

Recent research in Ireland may be showing that this is not quite the case. Scientists there have been studying invasive Mediterranean rhododendrons in order to figure out how they are able to achieve proper pollination without their specialized pollinators. Incredibly, it appears that these plants can detect when their pollination needs a boost and can act accordingly. Studies have shown that these plants are able to slow or even stop the production of nectar toxins in order to attract other pollinators—in short, if a plant is in its native range, it can afford to be more selective as its natural pollinators are most likely around. It seems that some rhododendrons are able to adapt quickly to a change in their normal pollinators.

While the chemicals present in a plant's blooms can be used to ward off unwanted visitors, there are a wide variety of different chemicals found in plants that have been found to actually help pollinators after a meal. Sunflower pollen, for example, has been shown to help bees fight off dangerous pathogens. Many plants seem to walk a fine line in their chemical brews, creating mixes that ward off pests or unwanted pollinators while also helping desirable visitors. In the grand scheme of things, these specialized pollinator relationships are risky as the effectiveness of close relationships also binds the two organisms together. Without their specialized pollinators, some plants are unable to attract alternatives and ultimately decline. The same can be true for pollinators that cannot find the plants they need. When you're thinking about what to plant this year, make sure to include plants that support the beneficial animals native to your area.

Pollen

Humans aren't the only species on Earth that affect the quality of the air. Beginning each spring, plants of every size, shape, and color throw countless pollen spores into the atmosphere. Whether by accident or design, plants release a huge amount of pollen during their lifetime. From spring to fall pollen makes up a surprising amount of the air we breathe. This is a reason that pollen allergies are one of the most common ailments during the growing seasons, affecting millions each year as their immune systems decide they've had enough and begin to attack pollen on sight. While allergies to plants like birch, oak, grass, and ragweed are commonplace and irritating, it is a small price to pay; without pollen most plants would not exist. Plants rely on pollen to distribute genetic information between each other in order to create seeds. Since plants themselves cannot move to their neighbors to facilitate this exchange, they travel vicariously through their pollen. Plants have worked for millions of years to develop pollen grains that are able to withstand extreme environments. Even though pollen grains are in some cases literally cast into the wind by the millions, each grain possesses a specialized shape and a durability that far exceeds anything you might find in even the most advanced SpaceX research lab.

Pollen, the male fertilizing agent of flowering plants, is usually recognized as a fine colored dust. Depending on the species of plant, this pollen is engineered to do specific tasks in order to reach a female reproductive structure. Many wind pollinated conifers, for example, produce pollen that is light and easily carried by even a slight gust. Wind pollinated plants release huge amounts of pollen into the air in the hopes that some will land on another plant in the same species. Most pollen allergies are caused by wind pollinated plants. Other plants, known as angiosperms, attempt to perform more efficient pollination by tricking animals into doing it for them. These plants usually create large, showy flowers filled with sugary nectar designed to lure in animals that then pick up pollen as they drink nectar. This is made easier by the fact that many angiosperms create large pollen grains with shapes that stick to almost anything they come into contact with. Most of these hitchhiking grains are larger than their wind pollinated counterparts and do not travel easily in the air. For example, goldenrod, a common animal-pollinated fall bloom, is normally incorrectly blamed for the allergies caused by the wind pollinated but more subtle ragweed active at the same time.

The shapes of pollen grains are so distinct that most plant species can be told apart by a microscopic look at their pollen. Depending on species, the appearance of pollen widely varies with grains covered in various spikes, hooks, bumps, and wings. Scientists trained in the identification of these tiny capsules are known as palynologists, and their work at understanding the compositions of pollen grains could perhaps help us engineer more efficient modes of storage and protection among other things. The genetic information contained in pollen is protected by a double layered wall that is heavily resistant to most corrosive elements. Imprints of these outer shells are found in fossil remains dating back over 400 million years ago. This tough shell, able to survive long periods of abuse as it travels, is not enough to protect against the hungry jaws of the many animals that rely on pollen for food, however. Beetles, butterflies, bees, wasps, ladybugs, ants, flies, and even spiders are among those dependent on pollen as a protein source.

While at first glance plants may appear to be listless participants in the landscape, do not forget that they are very active. While certainly easier said than done, the next time you feel the familiar itch or sniff of pollen allergies remember that in this case the ends more than justify the means.

Seeds

Visualize for a moment the typical late growing season for the plants in your area. According to their own habit, each plant has grown, achieved pollination through flowers or other means, and has developed a crop of seeds to ensure the success of the species next year. But what now? How does a seed-producing plant take the next step and disperse these seeds into habitable areas? Come to think of it, what exactly is a seed anyway? Here we look at some of the different types of seeds in the plant world and the ways in which they get around.

After successful pollination, the genetic information from ideally two different plants comes together to create an embryo. This embryo, once properly encased, is what we call a seed. Seeds are a relatively recent addition to the plant world. Ancient plants such as ferns thrived for millions of years using spores as a way to spread throughout an environment. Reproducing through spores is a time-consuming, delicate process that requires moist and shady conditions to work optimally. As plants evolved, they needed a way to protect their offspring as they found new and different sites to grow. Seeds are the perfect solution to this problem. Seeds give a young plant protection from the elements and predators, a way to get around, and in some cases enough food to supplement growth during the first critical moments after germination. They are so effective at protecting their precious cargo that recently scientists were able to grow a plant from a seed dating from around 32,000 years ago!

Seeds are packaged very differently depending on the type of plant that makes them. Some plants cram multiple seeds together and create large cones or similar structures. These plants, called gymnosperms, rely on forming seeds into specialized shapes to help protect them as they travel by falling or being carried by animals. Seeds like this were the first types to evolve and are common in many ancient plants. Gymnosperms do not supply their seeds with much food, however, and individual seeds lack a tough outer shell. If the collective structure of the cone is compro-

mised, the individual seeds can become vulnerable to hungry animals or the elements.

In more recent history, we have seen the rise of other plants, known as angiosperms or flowering plants. In angiosperms, the ovary of the plant in which the embryo forms hardens and turns itself into a tough outer shell. This shell is then usually packed with nutrients to give the growing embryo a leg up as it emerges. While radically different in their construction, both of these kinds of seed are robust and allow for plants to be transported much farther and more reliably than had ever been possible before.

Plants display an overwhelming variety of seed types. Some plants create seeds in shapes designed to take advantage of the wind, helicoptering and floating among gusts in order to reach fertile ground. Other plants yield tasty and nutritious fruits and vegetables to tempt animals into having a meal. The seeds contained inside then hitch a free ride as the animal moves as many seeds are tough enough to survive a trip through the digestive system. In fact, some seeds require an acid bath in the stomach of an animal in order to properly germinate. Bittercress, commonly found along garden edges in spring, exhibits an example of another method that some plants use to distribute seeds. These plants produce a pod filled with seeds, which at the slightest touch bursts open and throws its contents high into the air. On many tropical islands and beaches around the world, coconut trees are a common sight. This is mostly due to the fact that their seeds are nautical wanderers, able to float incredibly long distances over the ocean during storms.

Because of their seeds, plants have become some of the most well-traveled organisms on the planet despite their limited mobility. Take a look at the types of seeds in your garden this year, and if possible observe some as they begin their journey into the world.

Leaving the Leaves

Along with brisk air, apple pies, and warm fires, other highlights of fall include piles of dead leaves clogging gutters, choking plants, and turning walkways into a slip-n-slide. It's a good idea to clean leaves up from your walkways and gutters early while they are still fresh. Otherwise, they can turn into a thick and soupy mess that is difficult to relocate. While moving them around can be a chore, there are some practical uses for leaves on your property and in many cases you can simply leave them where they are—which is generally the best option for the wildlife around you. Even if you've already had to deal with leaves this year to some extent, let's talk about learning to love your leaves, or at least learning to leave them in certain areas.

First and foremost, try and keep as many leaves where they fall, as small piles of leaves supply native wildlife with winter habitat. This is actually very important. A large number of native insects, amphibians, and mammals use fallen leaves for shelter in the winter. In even the most manicured lawn, there are areas in the periphery that can benefit from having a pile of leaves left to its own devices. Interestingly enough, due to the introduction of invasive earthworm species to North America our forests are losing much of the leaf litter that they once had. Any opportunity to keep leaves on your property helps ensure that they can be effectively recycled back into your local ecosystem. If you do need to remove some leaves, or relocate them, let's look at choices of the most environmentally friendly leaf-herding equipment.

A rake is probably enough for most properties unless you have difficult terrain. As with all hand tools, make sure the head is solidly secured to the handle. You don't want any wimpy tools that will fall apart after a few uses. Many areas can be cleared using a good rake, and unless the situation is dire, try not to bring in the leaf blower. Although they save time and effort, there are some pretty large drawbacks to using leaf blowers. The environmental effects of noise and air pollution due to powered leaf blowers is an area of hot debate. Recent studies have shown that running a commercial gas-powered leaf blower for an hour is equal in air pollution to driving a 2016 Toyota Camry for over 1,000 miles. The loud sustained noises from blowers can also have negative impacts on the local wildlife in an area as well. If you have no other option, then I recommend using backpack leaf blowers only as a last resort, and if truly needed, check out the electrical options over gas powered.

After all of your gutters, walkways, and/or lawn are clear, you may find yourself with a pile of leaves. After attempting (and possibly failing) to resist jumping into it, you can put those leaves back to work into making your property look and function great. Leaves can be used as an excellent mulch that will quickly be recycled back into your soil. Keep this mulch 2-3 inches thick, and use it to insulate the soil around plants over the winter and to help with weed control in the early spring. Piles of leaves at the base of shrubs can serve as homes for rodents in the winter and can give them a very easy time of nibbling on your plants if they see fit, so make sure leaves aren't in direct contact with the base of your shrubs and small trees.

As mentioned earlier, there are some areas of your property that you will want to clear of leaves as soon as possible. Brush leaf buildups from your gutters and install screens to help keep leaves from getting lodged in the system. Clogged gutters are easy to overlook and are a prime cause of roof leaks. Never underestimate the slippery nature of a wet leaf; get your walkways cleared ASAP. If you have a grass lawn, leaves will starve your grass of light and eventually damage it. You can run over the leaves with a push mower and shred them, as shredded leaves can get to the soil and feed your lawn, or you can remove them with a rake. I encourage you not to bag them up, however, and instead put them to good use serving the plants and wildlife in your area.

The Positives of Pest Damage

Throughout their lives, plants are constantly creating chemical concoctions and storing them in their cells. Commonly referred to as phytochemicals, these chemicals come in a wide variety of types, from the aromatic and ant-warding menthol made in mints to the alkaloids present in lupins that make them too bitter for most grazing animals to bother with. One of the most common reasons plants make chemicals is for defense, and many of the chemicals formed in plants are produced in order to make themselves less palatable and in some cases poisonous to pests. Many colorful fruits and vegetables receive their tints through phytochemicals as well. Scientists have found that many of these chemicals can offer additional health benefits to humans. The phytochemicals present in garlic, for example, produce a strong aroma when released through damage that wards off insects, fungi, and other dangers. These same phytochemicals have also been found to be beneficial to the cardiovascular system while they help the body fight off cancer at the same time. Phytochemicals found in pine trees are widely used to make solvents such as turpentine as well as in cosmetic products. Hops not only lend their signature bitterness to beer, they also release phytochemicals into the brew that aid in preventing unwanted bacterial growth. Many of these phytochemicals are also antioxidants and help prevent damage caused by unpaired oxygen atoms that can disrupt cells in our body. Interestingly, studies are beginning to show that many of these phytochemicals work in combination with each other to offer different health benefits to our bodies upon consumption.

Individuals who eat a diet with an abundance of fresh fruits and vegetables have been found to have healthier cardiovascular systems and also lower incidences of cancer. These same findings have not been seen in studies of people who take many of the same basic antioxidants and other chemicals alone and in synthetic form. In short, it seems that antioxidants and other phytochemicals react with each other in fruits and vegetables to become more beneficial when consumed together. As the amount of fresh fruits and vegetables consumed increases, it seems that the benefits received increase as well, as a greater variety of these chemicals are able to come together and increase the effectiveness of one another.

Plants regulate the production of phytochemicals based on their current state—a blueberry grown in an environment free from the stress of pest attacks will actually have fewer phytochemicals than a blueberry that has to worry about fighting off hungry grazers. It seems that the more stress a plant endures, the more phytochemicals are produced as a response. In effect, often times the ugliest fruit in the basket is also the most nutritious. A Cambridge review in 2014 found that fruits and vegetables grown organically had up to 40% more antioxidants than those grown using other methods. This is thought to be due to the increased amount of pests present in such operations. To a certain degree, it is actually beneficial to have pests in and around crops since their presence tends to create food that is more nutritious and beneficial to the human body. As you observe the various munchers and nibblers on your garden throughout the season, remember that they contribute to making your plants and produce richer in healthy plant chemicals.

Establishing a threshold for pest damage rather than attempting to eliminate pests entirely is an important first step in responsibly controlling them in and around your garden. In many situations, designing a garden that attracts natural predators and other beneficial insects is enough to provide natural and effective pest control. While damage from pests may seem unsightly, in truth grazing alone rarely causes mortal damage to a plant. Instead, many times it actually makes the fruits of your labor even more valuable.

Festive Parasites

One of the most common traditions during Christmas time is hanging mistletoe above a doorstep. The pastime is mentioned in countless books, songs, and movies as bringing good luck and possibly a winter kiss. This practice actually stems far back into human history. Mistletoe grows high in trees and stays green long after other plants have gone bald for the winter, and it has been viewed as a mysterious symbol of resilient life and fertility by many who have found its lush patches upon seemingly dormant trees or shrubs. Historical evidence points to mistletoe being used all over Europe for rituals by ancient people such as Celtic druids, Greek and Roman revelers, and Nordic orators. While it is no longer used to conjure up spells of fertility and vitality, the ancient beliefs in the evocative qualities of mistletoe have clearly been carried into our modern times to some extent. But while many still use mistletoe as a symbol for radiant mirth and holiday joy, in truth mistletoes are far closer to the Grinch when it comes to how much they give and take.

Although they do possess functional leaves and perform photosynthesis, mistletoes get most of their nutrients from another source. Rather than taking the normal route of gathering water and nutrients from the soil, mistletoe plants prefer to steal that which has already been gathered. Relying on specially adapted root-like systems, mistletoes latch onto specific host plants and become immobile parasites. Many times, such parasites do little damage to their host plants, and lab results have shown that some species actually latch onto the healthiest hosts possible in order to avoid causing mortal wounds. In the winter, some types of mistletoe also transfer energy back to their host to help them through the cold.

Clumps of mistletoe are also incredibly beneficial to birds, who use the masses for nesting and consume the berries. Studies on bird populations have found direct correlations between the amount of mistletoe in an area and the number of birds, especially predators such as owls and hawks. Mistletoes have been found to be extremely beneficial to insect pollinators who use them for food and shelter. Several types of hairstreak butterflies only use mistletoe to raise their young, for example. Many backyard mammals also rely on mistletoe for food during harsh winter months. The unique way that mistletoes shed their leaves before draining their contents, unlike most other plants, also encourages nutrient rich and vibrant forest floors. Birds are usually the prime spreader of mistletoe as they distribute its sticky seeds throughout a forest. Once a seed sticks to a plant, it grows on its own for up to a year until it finally taps into the host.

While the mistletoe of antiquity is a European species, there are two species native to the states that can be commonly seen, especially in winter when many host plants have lost their leaves. American mistletoe, for example, can most commonly be seen on pecan, hickory, oak, black gum, and red maple trees. These green spheres high in the canopy can be easy to spot from a distance. Trees in the open and exposed to full sun are especially susceptible to mistletoe attachment. Dwarf mistletoe prefers conifer trees and is usually seen farther north. This species at one point must have found birds sub-par at seed distribution, since it has evolved to have fruit that builds up high pressures and explodes, shooting seeds to other locales. Keep your eye out next winter and see if you can spot any mistletoe growing in the trees around your area.

Poison Ivy

Poison ivy is one of the few plants capable of making even the toughest bushwhacker quickly change direction. Almost everyone knows why—the typically glossy leaves, arranged in characteristic groups of three, exude oils and resins after they are crushed or disturbed. Once on human skin, a mix of compounds called urushiol goes to work, attaching to human skin cells and tricking the body's immune system into attacking itself. Humans are one of the very few animals affected by these compounds, leading scientists into thinking that they are not a defensive adaptation of the plant. Rather, humans are basically allergic to compounds that poison ivy utilizes in order to better retain water as well as ward off microbial pests. This is pretty unfortunate for gardeners and forest explorers, as urushiol is found in every part of poison ivy. Only a tiny amount is needed to trigger a reaction. It would take less than an ounce of urushiol to affect the entire human population. These compounds can stay on surfaces and dead poison ivy vines for years, so caution is required when working around areas with resident populations. I encourage you to allow poison ivy to grow wherever possible, however, as this plant has many benefits that are usually neglected.

Poison ivy grows well in a wide variety of locations and is an important pioneer species when areas are damaged through natural disasters or other means. There are several forms of poison ivy native to the United States, with Western North Carolina being a mixing ground for several different species. They are usually apt to take a vining habit, using their bigfoot-level hairy vines to grip onto trees and in some cases even become parasites of their supports. Poison ivy can also grow in areas without trees or other structures, and grows into small shrubs if conditions are right. While most Americans today don't give poison ivy any positive second thoughts, in the 1600s Europeans were mystified by the strange plants constantly being discovered in the New World. Poison ivy was one of those highly sought after 'new' plants, and several impressive specimens can still be viewed in some of the most garish and cultivated gardens of England and France. It is of the writer's opinion that modern American gardens should take a similarly inviting approach to these native vines. A landscape's resident wildlife would certainly benefit from such a change.

    While we are quick to keep a healthy distance, a wide variety of other animals rely on poison ivy for food and shelter. Multiple insect species raise their young in the lush foliage of the vines. The subtle green and white flowers of poison ivy are attractive to a wide variety of pollinators as well. Honey bees can even make poison ivy honey that thankfully lacks any ability to cause itchy irritation. After they are pollinated, the flowers lead to large clusters of berries that are important food sources for birds over the winter months. Larger animals such as rabbit, bear, and deer also enjoy munching on poison ivy whenever possible. In some cases, having a healthy patch of poison ivy nearby can deter deer from eating other more delicate plantings, as deer seem to prefer the taste of poison ivy over most other plants. Although it can certainly be irritating to human skin, poison ivy is a real benefit to the native wildlife in an area. By leaving small out of the way areas of poison ivy alone, it can be easy to supply some reliable and maintenance-free food and habitat for struggling native wildlife populations.

Chapter Three

OUR ANIMAL FRIENDS

Turtles and Tortoises

Turtles and tortoises represent some of the last survivors of ancient worlds long past. These are some of the oldest living creatures on earth and have remained relatively unchanged by evolution for millions of years. Turtles are generally classified as species that live all or part of their lives in the water while a tortoise prefers life on land. There are a few exceptions to this ruling, such as the box turtle which is called a turtle despite living on dry land. Basically, tortoises are turtles that decided to permanently move to dry land. The subtle differences between turtles and tortoises are of small consequence when describing the interesting and unique adaptations that both of these creatures possess, however. As a way to ward off potential injury from predators and other sources, turtles and tortoises have developed thick outer shells made of bone. Turtle shells are not a single bone; similar to our skulls, they are made of 60 individual bones that are fused together. This allows for almost complete coverage of the turtle's top and bottom. These outer shells are attached to the animal's spine and rib cage, allowing them to easily take this home-grown armor with them wherever they roam, which can actually be surprisingly far.

Despite their reputation of being slow, turtles and tortoises can really get around. Tortoises can traverse up to four miles of desert or forest a day while consuming any suitable plant or insect they come across. Sea turtles, on the other hand, swim thousands of miles a year in the pursuit of feeding and nesting sites. Other turtles prefer a more sedentary life, such as the common snapping turtle. When they aren't holding up traffic, these large turtles often lie in wait for any small prey they can get their powerful jaws on. Wood turtles also prefer to let their prey come to them, mimicking the sound of falling water by stomping their feet in a type of rain dance that tricks earthworms into coming to the surface. While some turtles may not travel more than a few hundred yards from their nesting sites, a pair of Russian tortoises survived a trip around the moon and back in the 60s, making them one of the first and few Earth species to complete such a journey.

Hungry sailors in the 1800s also helped tortoises embark on distant (one-way) trips when they filled their hulls with giant tortoises found on the Galapagos Islands and used them for food. Because of their innate toughness, tortoises were able to be stored on ships for long periods of time with little to no food or water. Although sad to think about, this truly displays the toughness of these creatures. A recent example of such spartan living was displayed when a red foot tortoise in Brazil was found alive and well in an attic after being locked away for 30 years, seemingly able to survive on termites and condensation alone. These tough animals are also able to hold their breath for long periods of time. Sea turtles can sleep underwater for up to 7 hours, while tortoises are forced to release the air in their lungs in order to hide in their shells.

Many of the turtles in the southeast U.S. are aquatic, feeding on plants and small animals in bogs, rivers, and lakes; most live for around 50 years. The commonly seen eastern box turtle, the state reptile embodying North Carolina's slow yet persistent walk towards greatness, is our only truly terrestrial turtle. Try not to move these animals far if you find them—they have an incredible urge to return to their home turf and are more likely to cross roads or other hazards once moved.

Avian Aviation

Every fall and winter, diverse groups of animals undertake a yearly migration leading them to warmer and richer landscapes while they wait for the spring. Many of these animals utilize incredible skills that help them find their way during these travels. While certainly not the only group of animals that migrate, birds take migration to a new level. In fact, the Arctic tern holds a migratory distance record that is over three times that of the humpback whale, the mammal highest on the list. Arctic terns travel over 40,000 miles each year following desirable weather and food sources. That is the same as going around the world over one and a half times! While most birds do not possess this extreme level of wanderlust, around 40% of the birds on Earth embark on yearly migration journeys. The vast majority of these migrations are undertaken to avoid cold and desolate winters, leading to most birds in the northern hemisphere flying south for the winter while birds in the southern hemisphere fly north. To accomplish this task, birds employ titanic feats some of which we are still trying to fully understand.

Birds are some of the most successfully brazen explorers of our planet. Clad in a lightweight yet protective suit of feathers, these animals are well-suited for survival in a huge variety of environments. There are Antarctic penguins that can survive temperatures as low as minus 120 degrees Fahrenheit, while desert-dwelling doves barely break a sweat in temperatures of 115 degrees Fahrenheit (birds do not actually sweat). Most birds also employ their signature skill of flight to great effect. There are birds that can fly up to 60 mph, and birds have even been recorded flying as high as 37,000 feet. These traits are all well and good, but they pale in comparison to the mechanisms that these animals use in order to navigate long distances.

Migratory birds have developed a navigation system that puts our own GPS systems to shame. Birds such as Canada geese, ruby-throated hummingbirds, and American coots travel through the southeast U.S. during the fall and winter using multiple skills and adaptations. As far as scientists can tell, birds employ three main methods to help them gain a directional edge. First and foremost, it is thought that birds use visual cues such as the sun, stars, and landmarks like mountains to help figure out where they are heading. These birds are able to synthesize and remember visual cues with a surprising amount of clarity. For example, laboratory tests performed on crows show that they are able to remember things as complex as individual faces for years. It is thought that many other birds also have impressively effective memories.

Birds combine this mental map with several other fine-tuned adaptations. They are equipped with a compass of sorts in the form of small amounts of iron in their inner ear. Scientists believe this can help them discern which way North is located. It is also thought that the nerve running through a bird's beak, known as the trigeminal nerve, detects subtle differences in the Earth's magnetic field. Since the Earth's magnetic field is strongest at the poles and weakest at the equator, this allows birds to further fine-tune their direction. Recent studies have also identified a specific protein found in the eyes of birds that is thought to give them the ability to actually see the magnetic field itself!

With the use of these skills, birds navigate the planet in unrivaled ways. Although a cheery and beautiful addition to any landscape, do not forget that they are also some of the most amazingly fine-tuned travelers the world has ever known.

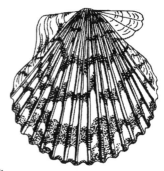

Bivalves: Nature's Water Filters

On ocean floors and river beds, colonies of organisms clad in armor plating filter nutrients and minute organisms out of the water around them. These creatures remain in the same spots for years at a time and can siphon huge amounts of water throughout the course of their lifetimes. Tiny fortresses nestled among the rocks and sand, they are essential recyclers and filters for aquatic environments. These interesting animals, collectively called bivalves, can also be of use in the monitoring and restoration of damaged aquatic ecosystems.

Mussels, oysters, and clams are the most commonly recognized bivalves, however it is an ancient and varied class of animals. The vast majority excel at pumping water through their gills in order to grab whatever small morsels float their way. Oysters, for example, are estimated to be able to filter up to 30 gallons a day. To put this in perspective, a human-sized oyster would go through over 13,000 gallons of water a day. Mussels can't match the individual pumping power of an oyster but they are able to pack themselves much tighter together. This gives them the ability to pick through a huge amount of H_2O; according to the United States Geological Survey, it takes resident invasive zebra mussels less than a month to filter through Lake Erie's 115 cubic miles of water.

The gills in these bivalves are extremely delicate and fine-tuned filters that are able to gather very small organisms and other nutrients from the water around them. They are not picky eaters; some fish farming operations are actually using certain types of mussels to consume fish waste that could otherwise pollute local waterways.

Because of the intricate nature of bivalve gills, they also gather many pollutants that are in the environment. Bivalves collect and store pesticides, heavy metals, and other pollutants and are capable of storing large amounts without ill effects. This makes them effective at measuring and combating levels of these pollutants in rivers and oceans around the world. Scientists in recent years have been using bivalves such as mussels as toxin sensors, observing the buildup of pollutants in their bodies and using it to gauge the level of pollutants in the immediate environment. These mussels are placed in areas of concern and left for a predetermined amount of time in order to collect pollutants. It's a testament to our current age of technology that I am able to write the following sentence: the mussels are then subjected to processes such as neutron activation analysis and atomic absorption spectrophotometry to gauge their levels of impurities. Using bivalves as pollutant sensors allows scientists to more accurately judge the levels of certain dangerous pollutants and helps give an early warning sign for potential contaminations.

Bivalves are also believed to have deep roots in the history of early America. Ancient American cultures extensively used mussels, clams, and oysters for food long before European settlers arrived. Many historians point to oysters as a main reason that New York City was able to grow into such a huge and successful city. The waters around New York City were at one point estimated to be home to around half of the world's oyster populations. These incredibly abundant and easily accessible shellfish made it possible for large amounts of immigrants to move into the city, safe in the knowledge that at the very least oysters were a guaranteed cheap food source.

America harbors a wide variety of native bivalve species. For example, North Carolina is home to some unique native bivalves including the Appalachian elktoe mussel, which beats out all other mussels, in my opinion, on name alone. Unfortunately, the vast majority of native bivalves including the Appalachian elktoe are imperiled. Studies as recent as 2004 showed that almost 75% of native North American mussel populations were in decline largely due to silt buildup from construction, agriculture, and other human interactions. Sediment from runoff is usually larger than the microscopic particles bivalves are used to dealing with and can clog the delicate filters on which they depend. Even a relatively small amount of sediment can degrade water quality, effect bivalve reproduction, and cover rocks that are usually preferred housing sites. Luckily there are many activists working tirelessly to preserve our native bivalves. Please do your part by not contributing to sediment runoff into local waterways, and give your local bivalves a better chance of surviving into the future.

Spiders

Although to some people the sight of a spider can creep them out, spiders are some of the most important animals in our environment. It is thought that spiders began their evolutionary history around 300 million years ago—millions of years before even the first dinosaurs reared their scaly heads. This amount of time has allowed spiders to develop an astounding amount of variations in the way they live. North America is home to over 3,000 species of spiders that we know of, and they are in such huge numbers that each acre of land is thought to be home to around 1 million of these silk slingers. Spiders are estimated to dispatch around 600 million tons of insects a year, making bats and birds look lazy in comparison.

All spiders utilize silk, however their uses are varied depending on the environment and preferred prey of each species. Some spiders create intricate webs to catch prey, while others weave silken tunnels for shelter and pursue their meals on foot. A few are even able to use small bits of web as a sticky catcher's mitt to snag passersby, and others actually throw bits of web much like a fishing line. There are spiders with such extreme adventure addictions that they create silk sails to hitch a ride on local winds or even on the electrical field of the Earth itself, traveling for hundreds of miles in search of a new web site. Going beyond even these intrepid arachnids, water spiders create air filled web bubbles that allow them to take up residence underwater.

Many of these feats are possible because of the resilience of spider silk—weight for weight, it is stronger than steel. Scientists are currently working on methods of using spider silk for multiple applications, including vests that absorb bullets while staying extremely light. Rather than raise populations of spiders to create the silk needed for further research and development, some scientists have developed a technique that is as fascinating as it is unnerving. By genetically engineering goats that produce spider silk in their milk, these scientists have been able to produce vast quantities of spider silk for their needs. Unfortunately the goats don't seem aware of the fact that they are the closest things to real life comic book characters on Earth at the moment—as of the date of printing they have not yet approached any production companies for movie deals.

While most spiders enjoy the outdoor life, there are a few species that are known to take up residence in our houses. In fact, some of the species of spiders that you find inside have been living with humans for so long that they cannot survive outside of a building. These spiders, while cobweb factories, actually provide your home and office with free pest control that is far more effective than any commercial treatment. The spiders in your home aid in reducing the populations of roaches, flies, mosquitos, clothes moths, and other pests around the house. Even though a few spiders with deadly bites have given their cousins a bad name, the vast majority of spiders can do us no harm. From a spider's point of view, bites are a costly affair which use up precious venom that could be otherwise put to better use. Because of this, most only bite under extreme circumstances.

There are written records of spiders taking up residences in Roman villas, however humans have most definitely coexisted with spiders in their houses for far longer than that. Many of the species found in houses have evolved ways to survive the unique difficulties in human house living, including infrequent prey and scarce water. While finding one of your spider roommates in the sink or tub can be an unwelcome start to your day, moving them to another part of your house will allow them to continue keeping other more harmful pests at bay. My preferred method of relocation is a glass or jar and a sturdy piece of paper. Once the glass is over your spider, slip the paper underneath and allow the spider to climb on top, sealing them inside. I encourage you to embrace, or at least turn a blind eye to, these ancient and helpful creatures as they in turn help protect your pantries.

Bats

As soon as the spring air starts to warm enough for insects to take flight, bats are also starting to come out at night. This is no cause for concern—bats are a huge benefit to the environment and perform a variety of necessary functions depending on where they live. In warmer climates, large bats feed on fruit and are some of the most effective seed distributors in the world. In fire ravaged areas, these fruit bats play a crucial role in spreading the seeds of forest plants. Other bats have evolved more specialized forms of eating such as sipping on nectar, hummingbird style. Then there are the well-known vampire bats, who have taken a liking to blood as meals and prefer to lap their food from sleeping cattle. In North America, however, the vast majority of bats eat insects.

Most bats in the States can be commonly seen around clearings and water edges, where they enjoy increased insect activity and can sometimes be seen skimming the surface of water for a drink. Insect eating bats generally use echolocation to ping the surrounding area and locate prey in the dark. They do this by blasting their immediate area with sound, produced from the throat or tongue-clicking, and listening to the returning echo. Some bats are even able to close off their ears as they do so in order to keep from going deaf. They then 'turn on' their ears in time to hear the echo. Bats are some of the most agile aerial hunters due to their incredibly precise echolocation in combination with their lightweight and flexible wings. When being hunted by bats, some moths have developed ways to detect the ultrasonic sound pulses produced by bats and react accordingly by either taking evasive action or by disrupting the signal. Studies have shown that certain bats have adjusted the frequencies they use for echolocation in order to keep up in this late-night arms race. It is important that they stay up to par, as the average bat consumes almost its entire body weight in insects each night.

While they can look a bit like flying mice, bats are actually more closely related to primates than rodents. Bats are thought to have evolved from tree dwelling animals that decided to jump onto prey from above. They slowly developed wings that were increasingly sophisticated, leading to the ones that they use today. The wings of a bat are incredibly thin and agile, allowing for much greater maneuverability than most birds. They also use their wings to 'breathe' in a sense. The surface area of a bat's wings make up a huge amount of the animal's total surface area, and allow for an efficient exchange of heat and gases which can take some of the burden off of the lungs during flight.

Bats in the southeast U.S. hibernate during the winter and do so in caves, large tree hollows, or other similarly protected sites. Interestingly, some will travel hundreds of miles from their winter homes and set up a separate residence in the summer. Bats return to the same roost year after year if possible, and are incredibly impacted by habitat loss. North American bats are also being wiped out by a fungal disease known as white nose syndrome. Luckily, some critical local hibernation sites have been isolated by authorities to help control the spread. Sites such as these can hopefully aid in the comeback of some of our endangered species. A few areas show some hope. Earlier this year the lesser long-nosed bat was removed from the endangered species list. This marks the first bat species to be removed due to a recovery in population. By providing bat habitat such as hollow trees and/or putting up bat houses, and by making sure the bats in our areas have plenty of insects to eat, we can help make sure they are not the last.

Frogs and Toads

Early spring is the time of year that the loudest singers of the night begin their songs. I'm not talking about crickets—as the weather thaws the frogs and toads in the landscapes around us are just beginning to emerge from their winter slumbers. As soon as it gets warm enough, sometimes as early as February or March, they gather around wet areas to reproduce and throw amphibian parties. Frogs and toads come in a variety of shapes and sizes. The smallest known vertebrate is a pencil eraser-sized frog, while the largest frog weighs in at over seven pounds. The Appalachian Mountains are home to a wide variety of amphibians, and is in fact known as one of the world's premier salamander habitats. However, for this note, we'll narrow our focus towards frogs and toads.

If the midnight serenades are not enough to endear your heart to frogs and toads, the benefits that they can provide to your property should do the trick. The primary diet of frogs and toads are insects, and they are great at keeping pests at bay. They are also important food sources for other wildlife including birds of prey, snakes, and raccoons.

To clear things up straight away, frogs and toads belong to the same family but have some slight differences. Both spend the first part of their lives as tadpoles, however toads usually have thick, dry skin compared to frogs. Frogs generally prefer to live near water and possess huge hind legs useful for propelling them towards safety. Toads, on the other hand, do not have such powerful legs and rely mostly on camouflage to hide from predators. Toads and frogs both possess glands that secrete bitter or poisonous substances to ward off attackers. These creatures are able to breathe through their skin, and in some cases don't even need their lungs to survive. Toads like the southern toad and fowler's toad have knobs on their feet to help them dig down into the soil to overwinter, while aquatic frogs spend their winters under water. Some frogs, like the early rising spring peepers and wood frogs, can survive being frozen for prolonged periods of time. They do this by pumping glucose throughout their bodies and dehydrating their organs. Once the spring thaw rolls around, these frogs can be ready to chirp in just a few hours. And that's pretty important, as the sounds frogs and toads make are critical to their reproduction.

Their calls not only help other amphibians locate sources of water—female toads and frogs also use the calls of potential suitors as a way to find the best mate. The most desirable calls are the deepest, most resonant bellows. Many frogs and toads have unique adaptations that help amplify their calls, helping these articulate amphibians call at ridiculous volumes—the loudest frog can reach noise levels higher than a lawn mower.

There are an alarming amount of declining plant and animal species throughout the world, including amphibians. These declines are partly due to human actions. Scientists have noticed that frog and toad numbers worldwide have been decreasing at a rapid pace for years. This is thought to be due in part to pollution, loss and fragmentation of habitat, and the spread of a parasitic fungus throughout the world's amphibian species. Luckily European engineers seem to have perfected toad tunnels under highways that reduced amphibian roadkill by upwards of 90% in the areas where they were implemented. Hopefully we will see similar wildlife roadways spring up all across the states as well. There are some easy things that you can do to help the frogs and toads in your area. Leave logs and rocks on your property wherever possible to provide amphibian shelter, along with tufts of sedges and grasses. A recent study found that toads grew to much larger sizes when living in an area with fleshy fruits—try planting a native species such as an American plum to give the frogs and toads in your area a boost. For the aquatic species in your area, having a small pond (or even a deep enough puddle) can help certain species of frogs looking for water in which to lay their eggs in late winter and early spring. As always, pay attention to what you spread into the environment around you as frogs and toads are especially susceptible to common household runoff such as pesticides, oils, and paints due to the fact that they absorb them readily through their skin. By following these steps, you can go a long way in ensuring a healthy population of frogs and toads in your area.

Earthworms

The ground around us is riddled with a hidden network of tunnels, crossing every which way and hidden from sight. While humans have been the creators of some elaborate tunnels including the 30-mile Channel Tunnel linking England to France and the New York City subway system, which costs millions of dollars a year simply to maintain, as far as tunnel making goes we are quite subpar compared to other burrowing animals. In fact, the world's most effective and important diggers are well known to nature lovers and city slickers alike. Earthworms of all shapes and sizes are constantly moving throughout much of the soil, tunneling their way underneath garden and turf, improving soil health as they go. While some might negatively view earthworms based on their slimy and wriggly appearance, exercise restraint when judging them based on their wormy demeanor. If it wasn't for earthworms, our soil and in effect the world as we know it would be very different indeed.

Earthworms are some of the main contributors to soil tunneling. It is estimated that the average yard in the U.S. is home to over 900,000 earthworms. Earthworms are split up into three groups depending on where they live, with some living in leaf litter and compost at the very surface of the soil, some burrowing down into permanent burrows over six feet deep, and the rest taking up residence in the first foot or so of soil. Feeding on microscopic organisms and decaying matter in the soil, earthworms are constantly eating as they go, and at the same time constantly pooping. This is a good thing, however, as the waste worms leave behind is incredibly high in nutrients. Very simply, earthworms condense many of the nutrients in decaying matter such as leaf litter and leave them behind worked into the soil. Earthworms are also full of microorganisms, and as soil passes through them a few of these microorganisms are left behind, where they are of great benefit to soil health. Many plant roots love earthworm tunnels as they are basically areas of loosened, nutritious soil. Stormwater is also able to percolate through the soil using these tunnels, and studies have shown that having enough earthworms in an area contributes greatly towards reducing stormwater runoff. Earthworms primarily feed in areas rich in decaying matter on top of soil. An easy way to promote populations of earthworms in your area is to leave leaf litter wherever possible. As the leaves decay over the following season, you will be surprised at the number of earthworms showing up to provide your property with free fertilization.

There are estimated to be over 180 earthworm species currently found in the U.S., however a good deal of the country's resident earthworm populations were wiped out in the last ice age as glaciers scraped most of the topsoil from the ground. Many earthworms commonly seen in eastern American gardens are in fact European species brought over in the 1700s in the ballast of ships and as stowaways in plant deliveries from the old world. Some of these species seem to destabilize our native forest environments by quickly devouring piles of leaf litter and stashing their nutrients below the soil. Most native U.S. forests are not adapted to take advantage of this and so they end up missing out on the influx of nutrients. This is leading to many native forests having difficulty re-establishing areas of new growth as young trees are out competed by invasive plants more suited to a rapid flow of nutrients. Even though some invasive species can cause damage, it's undeniable that earthworms are incredibly important in the health of our gardens and landscapes. Taking a count of the earthworms you see in and around your garden can be a good way to judge the soil health. If you find your area lacking, try to introduce fresh compost into your soil to encourage some new tunneling tenants.

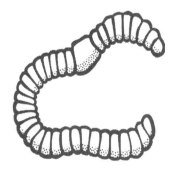

Opossum Appreciation

After the sun sets and we begin to head indoors, our forests and neighborhoods take on a new life as nocturnal animals make their rounds. One of the most misunderstood of these midnight wanderers is the opossum. While they are commonly known as ugly, stinky, and strange, opossums are actually a huge benefit to gardeners and the general landscape around us. Opossums are also one of America's true frontier animals. Their use as food and fur were a large part of early American life. Let's take a look at some reasons why opossums deserve a better reputation than they typically get.

Commonly called a possum (scientifically speaking true possums live in Australia), the cat-sized opossum is an ancient and unique North American native. It is the only marsupial native to North America, and like other marsupials the opossum carries its young in a pouch. Opossums are thought to have split from other marsupials in an evolutionary sense over 60 million years ago. This makes them some of the only mammals that have survived for so long, mostly due to the fact that they are incredibly versatile in habitat and diet. The Virginia opossum, the only opossum that lives north of Mexico, is thought to have moved into the states around 3 million years ago. Since then they have had great success foraging through the night for fruit, insects, reptiles, eggs, and basically whatever else they can find.

The word opossum is derived from an Algonquian word which roughly means "white animal." This white coat is one of the most easily recognizable traits of an opossum when seen. Opossums have more teeth than other mammals, however they will only use them in self-defense if absolutely necessary. While they may hiss and show off their pearly whites it is usually just a bluff. Instead, opossums prefer to play dead. When in extreme duress an involuntary response causes the opossum to fall down and stiffen. The creature's heart rate and breathing rate drop dramatically, but it is still conscious. If harassed further it is able to make itself smell just as bad as it looks. These tactics are usually enough to confuse and ward off potential predators. If you stumble upon a startled opossum, leave it alone with a clear path for escape and it will soon be on its way.

Most opossums forage and live in an area which can be as large as 50 acres. They are constantly on the move and usually do not take up permanent residence in any location, preferring the wandering lifestyle. While doing so, opossums are actually incredible allies in the fight against Lyme disease. Studies have shown that opossums are constantly grooming themselves in search of a snack. Because of their voracious grooming habits, each opossum is able to eliminate around 5,000 ticks each year. Opossums are also immune to most venoms and actively hunt any snakes they find. At the same time, they are always on the lookout for slugs, snails, and other garden pests. Opossums play a vital role in landscape cleanup and remove a large amount of spoiled food and trash from the environment as well.

Opossums are remarkably resistant to rabies and most you see are on the search for food. The best thing that you can do to keep them away from your house is secure your trash cans and don't leave food out. If you find an opossum under your deck or elsewhere, keep in mind that their wandering nature will compel them to leave shortly. Once they are gone, close up any entrances with hardware cloth.

Cardinals

The jovial cardinal is a common sight in eastern American winter landscapes. Forming close-knit groups during the colder months, these scarlet songbirds easily stand out amongst the whites and browns of a chilled backyard. While it may seem like cardinals are only in the area during winter, they do not migrate at all and are some of the most permanent residents of the forest borders of eastern North America. The cardinals you see in your area are very much your year-long neighbors. Most only live within a mile of where they were born, using their stout and powerful beaks to feed on a wide variety of seeds, berries, and insects. Even though they are easily drawn to bird feeders, especially ones stocked with sunflower and safflower seeds, cardinals also perform some critical tasks while hidden away in dense briar thickets and shrubs.

The cardinal native to eastern North America, the Northern Cardinal, is currently involved in controversy as some scientists are pushing for it to be split into multiple separate species. These birds originally had a much smaller range centered in the southeastern states. They have been slowly working their way northward, however, and with the aid of human-supplied bird feeders and urbanized forest landscapes cardinals are now common along the east coast all the way into Canada. This has led to their success in charming countless American bird lovers. Cardinals are the state bird of seven U.S. states including North Carolina, using their brilliant plumage to capture the attention of any wandering eye. Male cardinals are almost entirely red, including their impressive mohawk-like crest. The only exception is on and around their face, where they possess a black or gray mask. Females are a much more subtle brown overall with red and gray highlights around the crest and face. Male cardinal coloration is thought to be a way to judge a subject's viability as a mate—the brighter the red, the healthier the bird.

Recent studies into how exactly cardinals make red feathers has shed some light into the genetic makeup of many other birds as well. It seems that cardinals use carotenoids obtained through their diets to create their vibrant hue, however many of the carotenoids obtained through seeds are yellow. Cardinals utilize a specific gene to make an enzyme that turns these yellow pigments to red. Interestingly enough, scientists found that many other birds use these same genes in their eyes in order to help them see colors. It seems that in more ways than one, being red as a bird is simply a matter of expression.

Cardinals are believed to mate for life, and they use complex songs to communicate with their partner. Young cardinals are mostly taught songs by their parents, and these songs have been found to have regional dialects in different parts of the country. Even female cardinals sing, which is rare for a songbird. Usually, the female sings while she is sitting on her nest in order to let her mate know to bring back food ASAP. During child rearing it is the male's duty to keep the family fed. This can take a gargantuan effort, as their young are fed mostly insects at a rate sometimes approaching 10 times an hour. Cardinals normally have multiple broods per year, and they provide indispensable garden pest control through this feeding alone. Scientists recently discovered that cardinals are our allies in the fight against West Nile virus as well. It seems that these birds are very resistant to the virus and are a favorite meal for hungry mosquitos. By taking one for the team and being magnets for these insects, cardinals help to keep West Nile from spreading as quickly to humans. Thank your local cardinals for their service by leaving dense shrubs and thickets wherever possible to provide adequate cardinal shelter and nesting sites.

Tree Squirrels

This summer, my house was under siege by a squirrel. At every screen door creak the immediate area was pelted with several well aimed projectiles. It seemed the squirrel didn't take kindly to our intrusions into their yard, and attempts to oil the screen door allowing for stealthier movements were unsuccessful at stemming the barrage. Neighborhood cats and dogs were kept away from the borders of the yard as well, and I began to appreciate the tenacity with which the squirrel sniper protected my property. It was clear that I was not the only one who noticed, as our yard was soon teeming with a large abundance of animals all sheltered under this watchful eye in the trees. While I have always noticed squirrels in the landscape, I have never had an opportunity to view the bonuses of this behavior, which at first glance was taken as merely the tantrum of a grumpy rodent. Helped by this added protection, the wildlife in our yard flourished. My resident watch squirrel has relaxed the yard's security clearance for the winter, and I have decided to look into how squirrels live and the roles that they play in the environment.

There are technically many different types of squirrels, but today the tree squirrel will be the subject of attention. There are three types of tree squirrels around the southeast U.S.; American red squirrels, fox squirrels, and eastern gray squirrels. Gray squirrels are generally the most common, especially in cities, although it can be easy to confuse them as they all look similar, except for subtle color variations. All tree squirrels naturally live in the hollows of trees or nests constructed from sticks and leaves wedged into the crooks of tree limbs. They use these nests for shelter and rest any time they aren't out foraging for nuts, berries, bark, sap, acorns, and buds. They also hunt for insects and small animals in times of need, and are able to run headfirst down a tree by turning their ankles 180 degrees. However, their most well-known trait is hiding nuts for later. Tree squirrels do not hibernate and so they rely on a hefty store of food caches to survive the winter. Each squirrel is thought to bury thousands of snacks each season, showing remarkable wit while doing so, such as burying similar nut types and sizes in the same area to help remember their location. Studies have also shown that if a gray squirrel feels it is being watched by a competitor it will create fake holes to throw them off the trail. It is believed that most squirrel caches are eventually recovered, however the ones left buried are then in a prime position to sprout and become new trees. Squirrels play a huge role in distributing tree seeds, and also distribute a wide variety of mushroom spores. The abundance of squirrels in almost every environment makes them important food sources for a large number of predators as well.

While squirrels in urban areas can be seen as the invasion of a pest, in fact the history of squirrels in America is quite the opposite. Squirrels were routinely eaten in early America and were the most common pet here for quite some time. There were huge initiatives in the 1800s geared towards reintroducing squirrels back into cities where they were previously hunted out of existence. President Harding even had a pet squirrel named Pete that he would bring to meetings. While sometimes they can be a nuisance, squirrels work well at summing up the American spirit through their tenacity, charisma, and adventurous nature.

Salamanders

I am fortunate enough to call the Western North Carolina region my home; it hosts an incredible amount of biodiversity, especially in the Blue Ridge Mountains. Due to their age and varied elevations, these mountains are home to a large variety of unique insects, plants, birds, and amphibians. Some of the best examples of this are salamanders. The mountains of Western North Carolina and Eastern Tennessee are a salamander paradise—there are more types of salamanders in greater numbers here than anywhere else in the world. The name salamander refers to an amphibian that possesses a tail in its adult form. There are many types of salamanders, from the bumpy-skinned terrestrial newts to the mostly aquatic sirens. The largest southeastern species, known as mudpuppies, can reach over a foot in length and use external gills to breathe underwater.

Appalachian forest floors are also home to a great diversity of another type of salamander—lungless salamanders. These salamanders are thought to have evolved from aquatic amphibians in the streams and lakes in the area. Crawling upon land, they took up residence in the cool and moist mountain soil under rocks, logs, and leaves. The ecosystems contained along varying elevations in the mountains suited a variety of different species as they evolved over millions of years. They still prefer these locations today. Many Appalachian species, like the red-legged salamander and the red-cheeked salamander, are unique to the area. Lungless salamanders rely on wet skin to perform all of their breathing, and so they cannot travel far from streams or other wet areas. These carnivores have small home ranges of 50-100 square feet that they patrol at night. They look for food in the form of small insects and other prey, snagging it with their tongue and using rows of tiny teeth to dispatch the final blow. Like frogs and toads, salamanders begin their lives in the water as tadpole-like young. Their lifespan varies, with some living for over 50 years. During that time, they largely rely on underground tunnels made by rodents and roots to get around, using their front legs to sense the vibrations of any approaching animals and escaping if necessary. If they end up getting into a scrape, however, all is not lost. Many salamanders are able to detach their tail in the event of attack, leaving their hungry attacker left holding the bag. Some salamanders can regenerate limbs and even brain tissue. Research is being conducted on the specific responses that these salamanders' bodies have to injury that might possibly lead to medical treatments for humans as well.

Salamanders are fascinating and gentle creatures that can easily be seen under rocks and logs while walking in the forest. After finding and watching a salamander, take care to replace their hiding place as you found it and do not handle the little beast. Salamanders possess glands that can secrete poisonous substances when threatened, and it is generally wise to just leave them be. Interestingly they are thought to collect certain types of bacteria in order to help retain this toxicity.

A study on Appalachian salamanders recently determined that they have been shrinking in size over the last 50 years. This has been attributed to rising temperatures due to climate change forcing these creatures to use more energy to survive, however air pollution and other environmental factors may be playing a role as well. Salamanders are also under attack from a fungal disease that is also causing devastation in frog and toad populations. As with most native wildlife, leaving some of your property wild and untamed is usually the best way to support populations in your area. This leaves plenty of fallen logs, rocks, and leaf litter for salamanders to hide under. The incredible and unique variety of salamanders in the Blue Ridge Mountains, and across much of the United States, is yet another reason to tread softly as you venture out into the wild this year.

Animal Intelligence

Humans have a bad habit of judging the world around us according to our own perceptions. It is part of our nature to evaluate things that we come into contact with based on how they either directly benefit our lives or how similar they are to how humans operate. A prime example of this is intelligence. Throughout the course of evolution on Earth, animals have undergone a wide variety of adaptations that help them survive the turmoils of everyday life. One of the most impactful of these adaptations is intelligence. While humans have surpassed all other creatures on Earth in our ability to utilize our intelligence for various means, far too often we think of ourselves as the only Earthlings in possession of such faculties. Let's explore some of the surprising and unique intelligences present in the animal kingdom and how they differ from our own.

To boil it down, intelligence can be roughly defined as the assembly of mental abilities that allow a creature to solve problems through experience. An intelligent creature will learn from mistakes and victories, changing both itself and the world around it to better suit its needs. This is the critical difference between intelligence and instinct, as instinct denotes an action that is ingrained into an animal and is utilized without having been previously learned. It seems that instincts are generally more prevalent in animals with simple nervous systems, and that the more complex an animal's nervous system is the smaller a role instinct plays in their everyday motions. As research is constantly undertaken in the fields of human and animal intelligence, however, the question of what truly separates "higher intelligence" from the rest of the animal kingdom is becoming muddled at best.

Analyzing a creature's intelligence is not an easy feat. Many of the intelligence tests given to humans center on language and communication, which obviously don't work very well when applied to an animal that does not share our methods of communication. To combat this, animals are tested on their innate intelligence by completing tasks centered on changing normal routines and executing self-control. For example, recent tests on elephant intelligence centered on their having to pick up a stick that was attached to a mat that the elephants were standing on.

In order to retrieve their target, the elephants needed to figure out that their own body was preventing them from picking up the stick, which exhibits a form of self-awareness scientists rarely see in nature. The elephants that were tested passed this exam with flying colors. While tests such as these give incomplete pictures of an animal's intelligence, we have been able to glean some pretty incredible information about how certain animals use their intelligence to their benefit.

It appears that the majority of creatures utilizing a similar kind of intelligence to humans are social animals. This is thought to be due to the fact that social animals require a beefy brain in order to effectively communicate with each other and to understand communications coming their way. Chimpanzees, close relatives to humans, possess incredible minds. While roaming their jungle territories, chimps fashion tools, hunt cooperatively, and actively deceive and manipulate those around them in order to better suit their needs (pigs are also believed to be active manipulators). This points to these animals possessing some kind of self-awareness, or a theory of mind. In fact, studies with chimps have led some scientists to declare that the only true intellectual difference between humans and chimps is our complex language riddled with symbolism.

It is believed that chimpanzees started using tools around 4,000 years ago, and since then some chimp communities have expanded their arsenal to over 20 tools. This gives scientists a look into how early humans evolved to use tools to shape their environment. Intelligence is not only limited to those creatures closely related to humans, however.

The majority of social animals exhibit similarly remarkable intelligence. Dolphins, widely regarded as one of the ocean's prime social thinkers, exhibit intelligence despite having very different brains than the ones we have. In fact, recent studies found that some types of dolphin have more complex neocortex structures than humans. The neocortex has long been thought to be the root source of human intelligence. If some dolphins surpass humans in the size and complexity of their neocortex, who knows what thoughts are bouncing around in their heads. We do know that young dolphins seem to pick a unique whistle as their name. These animals then respond to their chosen whistle for their entire lives. Scientists also believe dolphins are able to communicate extremely effectively using vocal communication. Closely tied to the way in which dolphins can survey their environment using echolocation, it is thought that when a dolphin says something like "look at that barnacle" to another dolphin, it is actually sending mental pictures of the barnacle in question along with words. Wherein humans picture ideas in our minds as we receive information, dolphins could help each other understand communications by sending helpful images along with information.

Birds are other largely social creatures that display astonishing intelligence. Crows, for example, are thought to have intelligence levels similar to primates using a brain the size of a walnut. They have been observed solving puzzles involving tool usage, it is thought that they can remember specific human faces indefinitely, and some scientists show evidence that crows plan their days ahead of time. This is especially impressive given that crows lack a neocortex entirely. Other social birds, like the African grey parrot, are able to remember and use human words in the correct context. Marching to the beat of their own drums, palm cockatoos are the only animal known to make a musical instrument. In order to attract a mate, males retrieve sticks of specific lengths in order to create the perfect drumstick. They then perform rhythmic beats on hollow trees in the hopes that a female takes notice.

The large and complex brains that many social animals have developed allow them to better weather the challenges brought by nature. This does not mean that a larger brain equals more intelligence, however. It can be easy to fall into the trap of thinking that bigger is better in the world of brainpower. As more intelligence studies are done on animals with small brains, it is starting to become apparent that good things do indeed come in small packages. Termites and ants, possessing miniscule brains that can be described as little more than a lump of neurons, are able to accomplish tasks such as ventilating hives through unique architecture. Certain ant species have been observed following the same paths along forest floors every day for their entire lives, even teaching young ants their routes so that their trails can be inherited once they pass away. How they are able to do these things with such small brains is a subject of intense debate. Science is starting to show that some of the wonders these tiny Einsteins perform are due to the unique community structures of their colonies. By utilizing each individual member of huge colonies as methods of transferring information to the whole, large colonies of insects work almost like a giant brain and are able to remember and react to the experiences of each other as well as those of previous generations.

Mammalian brains are large in part due to physical restraints related to our equally large size, it is believed. Research on insect brains is beginning to show that they can be remarkably powerful with less space in between individual neurons than our own. This allows insects with tiny brains, such as bumble bees and honey bees, the opportunity to solve complex problems. Surprisingly, bumble bees are thought to utilize simple emotions and complex navigational skills, and even pass on skills to younger generations. Recent studies have also shown that bumble bees are able to solve problems using skills that they learn through experience. In laboratory experiments, bumble bees who were taught to move a ball onto a certain spot for a sugar reward surprised scientists when they began to invent new ways to solve the problem on their own. This shows that although these creatures possess a good deal of instinctual actions, they are also able to utilize their intellect in order to solve unfamiliar problems as well.

Honey bees, one of the most successful social insects, display modes of thought in their colonies that mirror the way in which our own brains work. While honey bees are able to solve simple problems using their individual intelligence, they also utilize a form of group think that helps them come to grips with complex or unexpected problems. When swarming, a group of bees will leave the hive with their queen in order to find a place to start a new nest. The swarm will quickly settle upon a nearby tree or sheltered spot, and then wait. The oldest and most experienced scout bees will leave the swarm and search for a suitable spot. Once they have found one, the scouts return and begin to advertise the location to other bees through a specific dance. Other scouts will pick up on the dance and check out the spot on their own. If it meets their criteria, those scouts will then return to the swarm and give the same dance. The swarm waits until the majority of scouts are all advertising the same location to make their move. Cooperation like this allows bees to work together in order to solve problems that might be too difficult for a single member. Studies have shown that our brains subconsciously vote on choices in a similar manner, constantly weighing the pros and cons of decisions without us even being aware of it.

Intelligence in the natural world can take surprising and unexpected forms. While the multiple intelligences at work around us are strange and powerful, one thing to take away from these examples is that we tend to over-simplify the difference between what is considered an intelligent animal and a dumb one. While many animals are able to accomplish amazing and sometimes unbelievable feats using their intellect, do not forget that these animals are also displaying qualities that we find relatable as they at times mimic our own thought processes. Keep in mind that while human-like intelligence is far more prevalent than you might think, there are probably many other types of equally interesting forms of thought that we simply are unable to fully understand at the moment.

Each animal alive today has earned its place in the world through a series of hard-earned adaptations that help it survive. It is becoming apparent that intelligence, in its many varied forms, is not a human-only adaptation. While we aren't the only creatures on Earth to possess a thinking mind, humans have achieved a level of intelligence that allows us to consider the past and plan for the future. In doing so, it is our responsibility to ensure that the currents of time do not overwhelm the host of creatures that inhabit this world with us. As our understanding of animal intelligence grows with time, who knows what we can learn from the massed thinkers in our landscapes.

Chapter Four

STRICTLY INSECTS
(MOSTLY POLLINATORS)

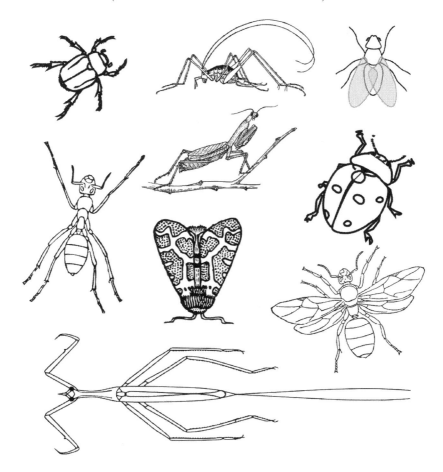

North American Pollinators Need Help Too

Although they are not native to North America, by now you've surely heard about the dangers facing honey bees; pests, diseases, and pesticide use have stressed the species to a critical point. These problems are in large part human made. Through their commercialization in both honey and pollination industries, honey bees have been exposed to a wide variety of stressors in large quantities and for extended periods of time. This threatens to make using honey bees for pollination services costlier and more difficult, in turn endangering billions of dollars' worth of crops. But did you know we have thousands of native pollinators in the states that are facing population declines as well? These native pollinators, especially native bees, are in general more efficient at pollinating than honey bees, are much less apt to sting than honey bees and other social insects, and are already living in the natural lands around us. North American native pollinators are the perfect solution to filling the pollination gaps left behind by struggling honey bee colonies. The future of honey bees remains in our hands, and luckily honey bee preservation is a major field in research at the moment. It is of great importance that we also work towards the preservation of our native pollinators at the same time—something you can easily do at home.

Honey bees were brought to North America along with European explorers in the 1600s. They came to a place already teeming with pollinators. Around 4,000 species of native bees are native to North America alone, not to mention the many species of flies, butterflies, moths, wasps, bats, beetles, and other animals that contribute to pollination. Many of our native pollinators are adapted to most efficiently pollinate our native plants; their life cycles are so finely tuned that they are usually only alive in their short-lived adult form as their favorite plants are in bloom. It will be interesting to see how changing bloom times due to climate change will affect these species and the plants they rely on.

Our native pollinators face some similar dangers as honey bees. Pests and diseases, spread from commercial or hobbyist beekeepers, have wreaked havoc on other insects as well. For example recent studies have found that Nosema, a common gut parasite in some bees, has spread from managed bumble bee operations into wild bumble bee populations. If you are a honey bee keeper, maintain the health of your hives in a responsible manner to ensure that you are not a part of the problem. Pesticide exposure also damages pollinator populations. Research has shown that even exposure to pesticides at levels that will not kill the individual, known as sub-lethal exposure, causes enough brain damage that learned skills are forgotten in bumblebees. Recent studies have also shown that pesticide exposure affects the development and longevity of ground nesting bees, which make up the majority of our native bee species. The assumption is that all pollinators are affected in similar negative ways when exposed to pesticides. As a matter of fact, a recent study found neonicotinoids, a type of commonly used pesticide, present in ¾ of the honey that was inspected. While the levels of these pesticides were below that listed as safe for human consumption, the effects that even low levels of pesticides have on humans are largely unknown especially in regards to long term exposures. It is time that we move past the common culture of 'spray first, ask questions later'. Surprisingly, homeowners spray larger quantities of pesticides than commercial agriculture. It is in every property owner's power to make a real change. However, if you have absolutely no other choice and must use pesticides, do so at night and while flowers are not in bloom to help keep pollinators from coming into contact with wet applications.

The last major danger facing our native pollinators is loss of habitat, both for nesting and feeding. Provide nesting sites for pollinators by leaving a section of your property untouched or put in handmade housing like a native bee hotel. Bare soil, dead trees, hollow stems, and reeds are all prime real estate for pollinators. Other great sites for pollinator shelter and nesting are tufts of sedges or grasses and piles of leaves. A good option is to put such areas in the back corners of your property, screened by shrubs or trees to ensure that they do not become eye sores. Keep in mind that some butterfly species require specific host plants for their young—an example is monarchs and milkweed. If you are looking to attract a specific species, research what their choice host plant is and make sure your yard is appropriately equipped.

For pollinator food, try and plant your garden in such a way as to have at least one plant in bloom at all times during the growing season—spring, summer, and fall. As mentioned earlier, our native species prefer plants native to the area, however most are not picky. Pay attention to the plants already in bloom in your area and use your garden to fill in gaps between them. Place your plants in groups of three to five. This forms a larger and more attractive site for pollinators than single plants farther spaced out. If your property is devoid of water, set up a bird bath or similar shallow dish with gravel at the bottom to act as a landing pad. Another option is to plant something with water collecting adaptations, such as a cup plant.

Our native bees are generally far more efficient pollinators than honey bees, for a variety of evolutionary reasons. These bees for the most part are solitary and cannot be moved around and manipulated like honey bees can. As such they can easily be forgotten when we think about the pollination of our fruits, vegetables, nuts, and other plants. It is becoming very clear that native bees provide a greater benefit to the world around us than was once assumed. In fact, it has been shown that it takes around 80 different species of bees to properly pollinate the fields of watermelons, blueberries, and cranberries in the United States. By paying attention to what we put into the environment and restoring some of the natural pollinator habitat that has been lost through urbanization, we can help to rebuild a network of pollinators that never needed the help of the honey bee to begin with in order to pollinate the foods we eat and the flowers we enjoy. Taking the steps listed above goes a long way towards re-establishing pollinator populations in your area, in turn building a healthier and more resilient ecosystem.

Carpenter Bees Do More Good than Harm

You know carpenter bees—the large yellow and black insects that bore holes in wood and can sometimes be seen patrolling their territories. These traits have given the carpenter bee a bad rap which it does not deserve. Carpenter bees are an important part of the ecosystem for several main reasons. These bees pollinate flowers, feed birds, and increase the yield of certain plant species. The damage they do to buildings is annoying, but many times only just that. The value of these creatures far outweighs the damage that they could cause.

Carpenter bees are the largest bees in North America, and because of that they are capable of some things that other bees just aren't built to do. Inclement weather that normally gets in the way of pollination can be overcome by sheer size. Rain showers and wind that would knock smaller insects out of the skies are shrugged off by these buzzing behemoths. They are also able to perform admirably in cold weather. These traits let carpenter bees pick up the slack in pollination during times when other insects simply can't risk it. Usually, their size is enough to scare away most pests and predators as well. This has led to carpenter bees being very docile—the females will only sting under extreme circumstances, such as being stepped on. The males, who can be see hovering in their territories around nest sites or flowers, will usually fly straight towards intruders at high speeds. While this can be intimidating, these males are in fact all talk and do not have stingers. Their large size also makes them easy pickings for hungry birds. Large bees such as carpenter and bumble bees are important food sources for birds and other animals, especially in spring where they may be active before other insects.

Carpenter bees have the ability to vibrate their flight muscles at specific frequencies while visiting flowers. These muscle vibrations trigger resonance frequencies in the bee's head and abdomen, turning the bee into a flying tuning fork. Known as buzz pollination, this vibrates the flower and dislodges pollen. Tomatoes, blueberries, eggplants, and cranberries all benefit greatly from this type of pollination and produce larger fruit in greater quantities when buzz pollinated. Carpenter bees are also able to recognize one another, and have been found to make it back home after being moved up to seven miles away. They generally live in semi-social settings involving varying degrees of cooperation between each other.

Two species of carpenter bee are seen around my home in Western North Carolina, the eastern carpenter bee and the southern carpenter bee. Both look similar to bumble bees with a shiny black butt—the southern carpenter bee also has a vest of red fuzz. These bees usually nest in the trunks and branches of dead standing trees in a forest. As forests are cut down and manicured, many of those dead trees are the first to be removed. This leaves carpenter bees with very few options for nesting sites. It's not difficult to see why our houses, decks, and barns look inviting to such a creature. Luckily there are some ways to make your property less appealing. Properly staining and/or painting the exposed wood on your property is first and foremost. While this will not guarantee that carpenter bees won't move in, it is much less likely if there is no unfinished wood visible. Paired with another possible nesting site nearby such as a pile of wood or dead tree, this may be enough to keep carpenter bees away. These bees prefer pine and cedar wood over other types for their nests. If possible, use another wood in your constructions if you have heavy populations in your area.

Even though the galleries that carpenter bees make in homes may look unsightly, the damage is usually not quite as bad as it looks. This is because carpenter bees usually excavate their tunnels in the direction of the wood grain, leading to little loss in structural integrity in the host wood versus tunnels in other directions. Many times the real damage comes from predators such as woodpeckers attempting to get into carpenter bee tunnels. I encourage you to rethink the commonly bad reputation of carpenter bees and pay attention to the active role they play in and around your garden.

Fireflies

Summer is the time for fireflies to come out; early June to mid-July is prime firefly mating season, compelling them to perform brilliant luminous displays after the sun sets. Despite being commonly called fireflies or lightning bugs, they are actually leathery beetles resembling many other garden beetles in their adult form. There are over 100 different species of fireflies in the United States, with almost 20% of those taking up residence in the Great Smoky Mountains. These mountains are home to some of the most unique firefly species in North America—an early summer stroll at dusk can lead to sightings of the local blue ghost firefly, the males of which keep their light on for minutes at a time as they search for females on the ground. The Smoky Mountain Synchronous Firefly, only just discovered in the 90s, is the only U.S. native firefly species that is known to synchronize light flashes with fireflies around them. Tourists are drawn to western North Carolina each year by the thousands in order to get a glimpse of these rare displays. Firefly viewing season can be elusive for some sightseers, as these insects only live in their adult form for five to thirty days. Interestingly, the majority of their lives are spent in a form far removed than the glowing hoverers we observe at night.

After a successful night of mating around the landscape, a female firefly will lay her eggs on the ground, under leaf cover or another similarly moist area. Fireflies start glowing at a very early age—their eggs even glow. After hatching, young firefly larvae are able to glow as a warning sign to any predators that they produce toxic and foul tasting chemicals. These chemicals help protect them as they live in the soil for up to two years feeding on snails, slugs, and other slow moving insects. While their young use bioluminescence as a defense mechanism, adult fireflies employ light for mostly one reason—to find a mate. Bright, over the top light displays can be a necessity when you only have a week or two to find a mate. Every species differs in the type of light display it gives off, however many displays are centered on males flashing into the night and waiting for a female to give a response. It is believed that female fireflies use the flashes from males to help judge their suitability as a mate. Depending on species, fireflies can produce light ranging from green, yellow, pale red, to blue, by combining oxygen with specific chemicals in their abdomen. The night time chemistry is kept in check as fireflies seem to use nitric oxide in order to precisely time their flashes. The bioluminescence that fireflies employ has been referred to as one of the most efficient forms of light in the world, as it gives off very little wasted energy in the form of heat.

Because fireflies live in the soil for the vast majority of their lives, they are extremely sensitive to changes brought through development and agriculture. Try to leave areas of your property untamed wherever possible and maintain areas of moist soil by leaving leaves and dead wood where they fall. Adult fireflies also appreciate long grass, shrubs, and trees for shelter during the day. Studies are beginning to show that fireflies are heavily impacted by light pollution as porch lights, street lamps, and other bright lights serve to outshine their light displays, and can make it more difficult for them to find a mate. Turning off any unnecessary outdoor lighting during firefly mating season can go a long way towards fostering local populations.

Bumble Bee Business

Bumble bees are one of the most common and easily recognized garden denizens. These large, fuzzy bees are active from early spring until late fall and are some of our most important native pollinators. In North America, bumble bees are some of the only native social bees, which means that they live in colonies centered around a queen who controls her offspring through various methods. This allows them to build small nests usually containing thirty to several hundred bees. Bumble bees are incredibly docile insects with an energetic personality focused on gathering as much pollen and nectar as possible. While they do so, these bees are able to accomplish some pretty unique things compared to other native bees.

Bumble bees are quite similar to European honey bees in a few of their nest habits. Bumbles are able to make both beeswax and honey, sculpting hollow orbs of wax which they use to raise their young as well as store honey for rainy days. They do not store large caches of honey, however. The colony dies off in late fall leaving new queens to spend the winter alone in fallen leaves or a similarly protected spot. This is one of the many reasons leaving leaf litter on your property wherever possible is so important. New bumble bee queens emerge in the spring and start a new colony, foraging and raising their young until there are enough to take over the outside work. Pay special attention to the bumble bees that you see in early spring, as they are probably queens.

Commercial growing operations have used bumble bees for pollinating plants, especially in greenhouse situations. This is especially true for tomatoes, blueberries, and other crops that benefit from buzz pollination. Studies on cherry tomatoes, for example, show that buzz pollination leads to an increase of around 45% in fruit production compared to other methods of pollination.

There are usually multiple species of bumble bees inhabiting a general area at the same time, and it can sometimes be difficult to tell them apart by coloration alone. This is due to a survival strategy that bumble bees employ known as adaptive color patterning. The bumble bee species in an area will tend to adopt and share colorations between each other, slowly looking more and more like one another. This is thought to have evolved to help them be more recognizable to predators; if all of the bees in an area have the same or similar warning colorations, a predator is more likely to have come into contact with the same colors in the past and avoid the associated sting.

While bumble bees have some of the most complex social structures of native North American bees, they also have some of the most complex cuckoo species. Cuckoo bees are species that have decided to steal from others rather than do the work themselves. The natural world has taken notice of the busy nature of bees, and every bee species probably has at least one type of bee or other insect that lives only to profit off of their hard work. Bumble bee cuckoos are varied in their tactics. Some even specialize in invading active bumble bee nests, killing the queen, and physically bullying the workers into doing her bidding. On any given day, a bumble bee nest is subjected to more danger and intrigue than an episode of *Game of Thrones*.

Bumble bees, like carpenter bees, are some of the only pollinators active in cold, wet, and dark weather. This, along with the fact that some native plant species like the bottle gentian are adapted to only use large bees for pollination, makes bumble bees incredibly important to the environment. Try and leave areas of uncut sedges or clumping grasses on your property to give them a place to settle down and build a nest. Bumble bees are attracted to a large variety of flowers—focus on having something blooming in your garden at all times to give them a constant source of nectar and pollen and your garden will soon be alive with the friendly buzz of these gentle giants.

The Wondrous World of Wasps

When the word wasp is thrown around, the image that usually comes to mind is an ornery insect armed with a stinger and angry friends. While this is true in some cases, in fact, overly defensive social wasps are the rarity among their kind. The overwhelming majority of wasps are docile, solitary insects and most don't even possess stingers. Wasps are one of the true invisible cogs of the environment, as they perform incredible pest control services while staying mostly out of sight. They belong to the same order as ants, sawflies, and bees—a humongous group of insects that together make up almost 40% of the total insect biomass on Earth called Hymenoptera. Wasps are present in almost every ecosystem, and they are believed to be responsible for around half of all insect-on-insect predation. In short, if it wasn't for wasps, we would shortly be overrun by a plague of not only pest insects but all insects combined.

Wasps have become some of the most effective killers on earth through several methods. Most wasps are known as solitary parasitoids. This means that they live alone, and their young feed off of other insects by living on or inside them, killing their host in the process. Like a mix between a ninja and a creature from a Ridley Scott movie, parasitoid wasps have evolved alongside specific prey for millions of years and as such know exactly how to place an egg on or in their preferred victim. They then leave their young to grow and use the host as free transport and protection, until eventually emerging to continue their lives. Some growing wasp larvae even manipulate their hosts into doing things they wouldn't normally dream of doing. A species was recently discovered that chemically manipulates its normally social spider host into leaving its community. These spider-puppets then spin web sarcophagi for the growing wasp to shelter in after its mobile meal is finished.

Fossilized parasitoid wasps have been identified in fly fossils dating roughly 50 million years old—wasps have been doing their thing for quite some time. There are thousands of species of parasitoid wasps that prey on all types of insects and other animals. There is a very good chance that for every pest you find on your garden, there is a species of wasp working its tail off as free pest control. These wasps come in all shapes and sizes but are usually very small, with the smallest known species being about as large as the period at the end of this sentence. Many of them possess an ovipositor instead of a stinger, which means that they lay their eggs through what looks like a stinger. Many wasp ovipositors are specially designed to reach the places that their prey live. For example some wasps, like the charmingly-named stump stabber, are able to penetrate through several inches of solid wood using their ovipositors in order to reach burrowing grubs inside. Ovipositors are unable to be used defensively, and as such most wasps are unable to sting even if they tried. These wasps are especially susceptible to pesticides, and by treating a pest outbreak with pesticides usually more damage is done to the beneficial wasps in your area than is done to the pests themselves. Exercise restraint when spraying for pests such as aphids, as sometimes leaving them alone for a few seasons can build up a population of parasitoid wasps that can keep pests in check completely on their own. Remember for every pest there is a predator more effective than a pesticide, and generally it is a wasp!

Another type of solitary garden patroller is the hunting wasp. These wasps also live alone, but instead of using a host insect as a nest of sorts for their growing young, hunting wasps make a nest of their own and provision it with prey for their young to eat. Most solitary hunting wasps nest in the ground, however some nest in wood while others make nests out of mud. Like parasitoid wasps, hunting wasps have formed close associations with specific prey. This allows them to instinctively know how to paralyze them with a single sting. The paralyzed prey is then taken back to the nest, where it is sometimes covered with a protective coating by the wasp designed to ward off fungal invaders (in some species, the egg itself exudes fungal-killing gases). An egg is laid on the prey and the room is then sealed off, leaving the unfortunate victim to watch as their new hungry roommate hatches and begins to eat.

Scientists have been able to develop some very interesting inventions due to wasp studies in recent years. Micro needles inspired by the stingers of wasps and bees are in development that promise to minimize the pain from injections, and labs are working on synthesizing new and powerful antibiotics from wasp venom. Studies have led scientists to believe that some wasps and bees can even recognize the faces of their nest mates, and decoding the way these tiny insects interpret faces could help us understand how our own cognitive systems work. While the sight of a wasp might immediately give you a start, do not forget that they are quite constantly performing indispensable services to the world around us. Most species are more defensive than aggressive, and will only attack animals that appear to threaten the nest, especially with social species like yellow jackets. While certainly easier said than done, if a nest is encountered slowly walking away will usually lead to a clean and simple escape.

The Ants Among Us

There are over 700 ant species in North America currently identified. Nature's premier foragers, they constantly mix nutrients and decaying matter into the soil to be readily broken down. They aren't working on their own, however. The small mound at the entrance of an ant colony hides a labyrinth of interconnected tunnels home to perhaps hundreds of thousands of residents.

Ants are the 'social butterflies' of the insect world—while there are other insects that live cooperatively, it is usually very rare. As far as we know, ants only live socially in colonies. Like other social insects, ants live in communities centered around a queen supported by a working caste of females. Males are few and far between, and exist only to reproduce with queens from other colonies. Some species have been found living together with similar species in shared colonies, and in some places ants have been known to form linked 'supercolonies' that can stretch for hundreds of miles! Ants are always mixing and aerating the soil, allowing water and air to penetrate to plant roots. They also help disperse the seeds of around 50% of plants—some plants even produce structures called elaiosomes on their seeds designed to entice ants to take their seeds back to the colony. The ants eat the elaiosomes upon returning home and discard the seeds into their refuse pile, effectively planting them.

Ants have been known to dabble in agriculture as well. Tropical leafcutter ants collect leaves from the surrounding forest, sending green trails all along the forest floor as they bring them back to the nest. The leaves aren't for the ants to eat, however. They are brought deep into the colony where they are used to feed underground fungus farms, which leafcutter ants have quite the appetite for. Leafcutter ants and their cousins fungus ants (who grow their fungus on pretty much anything) have been observed transporting fungus specimens to new nesting sites, and in the event of an ant battle enemy colonies have been known to take the fungi of the losing colony as spoils of war. Leafcutter ants create such immense farming operations that they produce huge amounts of greenhouse gases from their underground compost piles, actually rivaling humans in the impact that they can have on their immediate environment.

Ants also take part in insect husbandry, and a common site in a garden are ants herding aphids and other sap sucking insects together and protecting them from predators. They do this in order to have access to the sugary honeydew that their livestock produce as they feed. These industrious insects are able to survive all over the world, and they live surprisingly complex lives especially when you consider their very small brains. Ants possess a brain around 40,000 times smaller than ours, and while many ant feats are instinctually ingrained they are still quite extraordinary. The older ants of some species appear to teach young ants specific trails that they then follow for the rest of their lives. Ants have even been shown to have the ability to identify when they are infected with pathogens and isolate themselves in order to prevent the spread of disease.

Many ant species actively hunt for prey, and they are constantly patrolling the plants in their area and keeping them pest free. Some ants even make a honey-like liquid and use specific members of the colony to store their sweet brews. Many times, these 'storage ants' become so bloated and large that they are unable to move and are sometimes attached to the ceiling of tunnels like hanging bags of honey wine. It seems that ants take their cues to perform different tasks based on the frequency that they come into contact with the other ants around them. Much like the neurons in our brains, the activities of individual members of an ant colony are mainly triggered and changed according to the interactions with the ants around them. This allows an ant colony to form what's known as a superorganism, wherein the whole colony's behavior is shaped due to constant subtle changes in the schedules and movements of the individual colony members themselves. These changes cause ripple effects on the behaviors of those who come into contact with them, and over time the behavior of the entire colony can change in response.

While some species of ants are different colors, it can be hard to tell them apart. Many ants are most easily identified by microscopic features such as mandible size, tooth count, number of antennae segments, and so on. This is made even more difficult due to the fact that ants from the same colony can take different appearances according to their job. Soldiers, for example, are beastly muscle-bound hulks while the general worker is much smaller. There are even differences in appearance between workers, with some species having as many as three different worker types alone. This helps them perform specialized tasks very efficiently, however it can make identifying a particular ant species difficult.

There are several species that I will call out for being intrusive. The first are carpenter ants. These large ants don't eat wood, but they burrow through soft, wet wood wherever available. This can lead to structural damage in buildings that are affected. If you see these ants in and around your house, check for any structural or drainage issues that might have led to their moving in. The imported fire ant, becoming more common in the states, is another invasive ant in the southern United States. These ants can destroy and out compete other native ant species while packing a mean sting as well. Their extra-large nest mounds and bright red colors can usually give fire ants away. Contact your local extension office if you notice these on your property. There are native red ants as well, however, so make sure you get the right ant before deciding to remove them from your property. You want to leave the vast majority of the ants you see alone, however. Left to their own devices, the ants in the landscapes around us perform a huge amount of pest control, disperse seeds, improve soil health, and pollinate blooms during the entire growing season.

Attracting Caterpillars to your Garden

Butterflies and moths are not only a pleasure to observe in the garden, they pollinate plants and serve as food for a wide variety of other animals. Most gardeners jump at the chance to have these insects glide through their property as they sample what's in bloom and search for a mate. Caterpillars, on the other hand, are generally regarded as pests since their prime objective in life is to consume the maximum amount of leaves as possible. It can be easy to forget that these ravenous munchers hell-bent on the destruction of your plants turn into such a delicate and flighty final form. While it can be a tenuous balance between protecting your greenery and allowing for caterpillars to complete their life cycles, in most cases caterpillars will not inflict mortal damage on their plant hosts. In order to make the transition from egg to adult these slow-moving eating machines rely on a mix of stealth, trickery, and formidable defenses.

Caterpillars generally start eating as soon as they hatch, sometimes even eating their egg shell in the process. Gorging themselves constantly, caterpillars are forced to shed their skin multiple times during their lifetime in order to make more room for food. This is typically performed five times, and many caterpillars look radically different after each successive shedding. The spicebush swallowtail caterpillar, for example, disguises itself as bird poop as a young caterpillar but eventually mimics a snake after several molts.

Because they are so big and slow, many caterpillars have also developed other defenses beyond mimicry. Some caterpillars gain insect superpowers through the food they eat. Monarchs are a good example of this, since the milkweeds that their caterpillars eat imbue them with bitter and potentially poisonous chemicals. Tobacco hornworms raised on a diet of tobacco are able to fill the air around themselves with a cloud of nicotine when threatened, which can confuse or damage potential threats. Other caterpillars ward off predators by covering themselves with irritating and/or venomous spikes. Much like a cactus, if you find yourself on the receiving end of a prickly caterpillar a piece of tape works wonders at removing the hard to see leftovers. There are even caterpillars that go on the offensive and choose to spray attackers with stomach acid instead of relying on pure defense.

At the end of their lives as caterpillars, they perform what is probably their most famous feat. Depending on the type, caterpillars form a cocoon or a chrysalis and use that as shelter during their metamorphosis. This is when the caterpillar literally digests itself, turning most of its body into a protein rich goo. Special 'packets' of cells are left behind, however, and these specialized cells use nutrients in the goo around them to transform into the insect's final form.

Gardening for moths and butterflies requires consideration for the palette of their caterpillars. Most adult moths and butterflies are generalist feeders and are easily attracted by groups of flowering plants with compound flowers such as in the carrot family. In order for adult populations to stick around, however, a more directed approach is needed. Many species have unique plants in mind when it comes to laying their eggs. Most caterpillars only feed on a few select plants depending on their species. For many native butterflies, native plants are preferred over others for laying eggs and raising caterpillars. In some cases they are able to use non-native plants in the same family. When planting for butterflies and moths, some species are obvious in their main caterpillar host plants such as the spicebush swallowtail and pipevine swallowtail. For other species, check out this great list of host plants from the NC State extension at https://content.ces.ncsu.edu/butterflies-in-your-backyard.

Mason Bees

In early spring, you will often find the author loitering around a multitude of wood nesting bee houses scattered around the yard, waiting for signs that the first mason bees are emerging from their winter domiciles. I understand that for most readers this might not be the most exciting task, however let me tell you why mason bees are such fascinating and important native bees. That way, you too can rejoice as you see similar species emerging in the landscape around you during the spring and summer.

In the U.S. and Canada there are over 130 species of mason bee, however only 30 are native to the east coast. Mason bees frequently make their nests in hollow reeds, tubes, or holes in dead standing trees. They do not excavate nests themselves, instead preferring to use cavities that have already been made by other borers such as beetle larvae. It is easy to provide man-made housing for mason bees if there are no dead trees in your area. This is one of the reasons that some mason bees have been used in commercial pollination to great effect.

Like the majority of our native bees, mason bees are solitary, which means they do not live in a nest or share labor to support a single fertile queen. Instead, each female is a queen in her own right and provisions a series of rooms, commonly called cells, with the food her young will need. Once a suitable tunnel has been found in wood, mason bee females will check to make sure it's empty and then mark the entrance with a unique scent. While they aren't the only bees to use scent markings, the scientific name for mason bees, Osmia, refers to the fact that they use specific scents to mark the entrance to their nests. This scent will help her find the entrance to her nest while also letting other female mason bees know to keep moving. Our new homeowner doesn't take long to relax in her new space, however, and immediately sets out to gather a ball of pollen around the size of a pencil eraser. An egg is then laid on the pollen and the cell is sealed. She repeats this process until the tunnel is filled, usually around 12 cells per tunnel. The cells are sealed with different materials depending on the species of bee. Mason bees, in accordance to their name, use mixtures of clay, mud, sand, and small pebbles to seal their cells. Like other bee species, mason bees are able to determine the sex of their offspring and lay females towards the back of the nest with males on the outside. This allows males to emerge first in preparation for mating as soon as the females are ready, however it also ensures that any predators attacking the nest would eat the less important males first.

Mason bees are great to have around for several reasons. These animals are spring's true pollination juggernauts. They are active in very cold temperatures that make honey bees retreat to their warm hives. Mason bees are also very efficient pollinators even compared to honey bees. This is due to the fact that they do not carry the pollen they collect in tidy baskets, known as corbiculae, like honey bees or bumble bees. Instead, they prefer to dive right into blooms and cover as much of their body in pollen as possible. Many native bees also seem to approach flowers very differently than honey bees, and this causes them to come into contact with the reproductive parts of native flowers more frequently than non-native species. Because most of our native bees take a 'messier' approach, it actually leads to more pollen falling off of the bee and pollinating the plants visited. This can be seen best in apple and cherry trees, where one mason bee can do the work of 300 honey bees.

Not all mason bees are native, however. There are currently over 20 known introduced species of bee in the states. I have noticed the Japanese horned-face bee to be very common in my area. This solitary wood nesting species was brought into the states in the 70s by the USDA in order to assist with crop pollination. Unfortunately, someone didn't get the memo that we have plenty of excellent pollinators here already. While honey bees and other managed pollinators are used widely in modern agriculture, unfortunately large fields of single crops seem to be very disruptive to native mason bees. While large areas of crops are great for pollinators as they bloom, after their flowers drop, many times the fields then become largely devoid of nectar and pollen. Most of our solitary bees have small foraging ranges and are unable to pass through large areas of land in the search for food, and as a consequence many crop fields are not able to sustain a healthy population of native pollinators. By including areas of pollinator habitat mixed throughout crop fields, future farms will have the ability to harness the incredible pollinating power of these and other native pollinators; at the same time, they will also attract other beneficial insects that will be glad to offer free pest control.

Insect Mimics

One of the most powerful survival strategies in nature is the ability for certain animals to be poisonous or venomous. Both of these traits employ chemicals that make the creature toxic to others. Poisonous creatures generally use their toxins in a defensive nature—for example, many toads secrete toxins and are harmful when consumed. Venomous creatures, on the other hand, inject their toxins through bites or stings. These toxins can be very effective at distracting, disabling, or even killing the victim. Because of the effectiveness of natural toxins, these creatures are usually avoided by predators that are in search of easy prey. Some poisonous and venomous creatures have developed distinct colorations that help them in displaying their toxic talents. Poison dart frogs, lionfish, coral snakes, and black widow spiders are among the animals that have colorations designed to stand out from the landscape and other animals. In many situations, simply displaying these colors is enough to scare away most predators. This visual defense is powerful enough to attract the attention of creatures also looking for a way to defend themselves. Wherever there are populations of poisonous or venomous animals with distinct warning colorations, there are probably also creatures that mimic those colors. These nontoxic doppelgängers can adopt the colors and forms of their target to an impressive degree. One of the best ways to observe this type of mimicry, known as Batesian mimicry, is actually in and around your backyard this growing season.

Although primarily only used in defense, bees and wasps are well known for their painful and unpleasant stings. A good deal of our native bees and wasps have developed distinct warning markings involving stripes of blacks and yellows. You may be surprised to find that many of the yellow and black striped insects you see outside are in fact not bees or wasps, however. Many other insects have caught on to these warning signs and have adapted disguises of their own. Some of the major bee mimics are actually flies. Hoverflies commonly mimic both bees and wasps and can be seen flitting among blooms as they feed on nectar as adults. They don't eat nectar during their entire lives, though. The young of many hoverflies actually chow down on aphids and are a huge boon to the pest control in a garden. Hoverflies, also known as syphid flies, search for large groups of aphids and lay their eggs nearby. Some orchids actually mimic the scent of aphid congregations in order to attract hoverflies! There are many types of mimic flies, and while they don't all eat aphids in their young forms the pollination they provide is thought to be second only to bees. These garden mimics can usually be told apart from the real thing through a close inspection—mimic flies have only two wings compared to the 4 that bees and wasps pack. Flies also generally have larger eyes, smaller antennae, and lack the hairs that bees possess.

Another rare and interesting garden mimic is the fast-flying clearwing moth. Also known as a hummingbird moth, this creature looks like a mix between a miniature hummingbird and a fuzzy crawfish with wings. There are two species of clearwing moth native to the states, one which takes on the appearance of a hummingbird while the other tends to look more like a bumble bee. Both of these disguises serve to distract potential predators long enough for this agile moth to make an escape. Keep an eye out around viburnums and honeysuckles for a chance to see them as they zoom by.

Mimic flies and hummingbird moths are extremely sensitive to pesticides. If you do not see these creatures and routinely spray pesticides, you might be surprised at what visits once you slow or stop the applications.

Ladybugs

Ladybugs are one of the most common and easily recognized members of a landscape. There are thousands of species of these beetles worldwide, with over 400 that we know of taking up residence in the states. Commonly referred to as ladybugs or lady beetles, these little insects are truly in the beetle family. The colorations of ladybugs can be extremely varied, and usually consist of reds, yellows, oranges, or pinks. Some ladybugs have spots, some prefer stripes, and some don't have any additional markings at all. Their bright shells are a warning coloration that advertise their bitter taste to hopefully discourage hungry birds, frogs, wasps, and other predators from taking a bite. As added protection, many ladybugs can also create foul tasting and sometimes poisonous secretions from their exoskeletons. From a pest control perspective, ladybugs are some of the gardener's best friends, as they eat a wide variety of plant grazers and sap suckers in both their adult and larval forms. While the diet of some ladybugs is specialized, many eat a wide variety of foods including aphids, scale insects, mealybugs, and the eggs of pest insects such as Colorado potato beetles and European corn borers. It is estimated that each ladybug consumes thousands of insects in its lifetime. Even in their young and growing forms they can eat around 25 insects a day. Their success in hunting and consuming plant pests has led to several exotic ladybug species being introduced into the states, with sometimes unexpected results.

Because of their innate hardiness and voracious appetites, ladybugs were some of the first insects to be widely used in the biological control of agricultural pests. Australian ladybugs helped the U.S. orange industry fight off disaster in the early 1900s, while the commonly seen European seven-spotted ladybug found its way across the ocean years later and has established itself in landscapes throughout the country.

Many of the introduced ladybug species seem to coexist rather well with native ladybugs, however there is a certain species among them that is not such a friendly neighbor. Hidden among our backyard beetles is a monstrous intruder, a ladybug that dwarfs our native species in both size and appetite. Originally hailing from eastern Asia, the Asian lady beetle has established a strong population in the U.S. and Europe. Scientists believe the spread was started by shipping containers laden with hitchhiking adults over the last hundred years or so. Asian lady beetles didn't lose their stowaway tendencies when they arrived, however, and these are the only ladybugs that prefer taking up residence in houses to escape the cold of winter. If you find congregations of ladybugs inside during the fall, winter, or spring, chances are you have your very own local population of these tenacious beetles. Vacuum them up rather than giving them the boot, as Asian lady beetles produce a stinky and irritating liquid when squished.

Asian lady beetles do a very good job at eating a wide variety of insects deemed crop pests, and they are also remarkably resistant to pesticides. While this makes them ideal for an agricultural setting, studies are showing that these beetles are also disrupting native ladybug species. Asian lady beetles appear to harbor huge amounts of certain parasites that can be dangerous to native species, and they also feast on the eggs and young of native ladybugs whenever they can. Rather than attempting to wipe out these introduced species, I recommend keeping native ladybugs in mind as you tend to the garden this year in order to give the species in your area the best chance of survival. Stop using pesticides; instead leave small populations of pests such as aphids and mealybugs alone. Left long enough, these will most likely end up attracting pest control more effective and sustainable than chemical applications.

Bees in Winter

For all creatures the winter is a time of harsh temperatures, scarce running water and infrequent food sources. Insects have incredibly varied ways in which they survive during this time. These can range from building a weatherproof cocoon and camping out through the winter alone, to huddling together en masse in the crevices of trees and rocks. Bees as a whole exhibit a wide range of these different strategies and taking a look at their winter lives can give a good idea of how most insects survive until the spring.

The most successful bee at surviving the winter is undoubtedly the honey bee. Although not native to the Americas, these bees play a huge role in our agriculture industries and are the bees most easily housed, moved and manipulated by humans. Honey bees horde so much honey because the whole colony survives the winter and needs an energy-rich food source during that time. Clustering around their stores, honey bees take turns vibrating and generating heat for the greater good of the hive. Their ability to work together and make such large quantities of honey is very rare among bee species and is one of the prime reasons that they are so successful.

The vast majority of bee species do not confront the winter in the same way as the honey bee. As explored in "Bumble Bee Business," bumble bees live in nests of around thirty to a few hundred members, usually in abandoned rodent nests or at the base of grass tufts. The majority of the nest dies off in the late fall, however, leaving new queens to spend the winter alone under piles of leaves or mulch. These queens distribute a chemical throughout their blood that acts as an antifreeze, keeping them free of frostbite until the early spring. They then found a new colony on their own, doing the work of an entire hive for the first few weeks until their offspring hatch and take over most of the hard labor.

The majority of North American bee species are solitary, meaning they do not share their labor in a hive environment but instead each female lays her own eggs in isolated nests. Most species do this underground, by digging tunnels and creating rooms that are then filled with pollen and nectar. Once there is enough food, the bee lays an egg and seals off the room. Every species has a unique decorating sense. One of the main differences between solitary bee species is how they make these rooms—some line their walls with a waterproof substance, some use leaves as wallpaper, and others use mud and sand.

Each female repeats this egg-laying process around twelve to twenty-four times and then dies, leaving her eggs to hatch and develop over the summer months. As fall approaches, these young bees then spin protective cocoons and stay tucked in until spring. This cycle allows for solitary populations to have a relatively wide dispersal pattern year after year, however their life cycles are finely tuned to the temperature changes of the seasons around them. This makes them especially susceptible to climate change; as bloom times change due to global warming these bees may be forced to find new sources of food as they emerge in the spring. About 30% of solitary North American bees take up residence in holes in standing dead trees left by other insect larvae. By giving native bees in your area spaces to overwinter such as refuse piles and dead trees, your property will be alive with activity come the blooming season.

Chapter Five

HUMAN INNOVATION & IMPACT

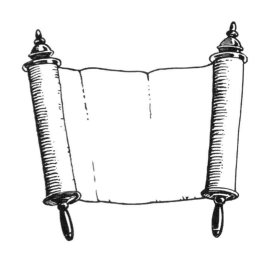

Paper

As you begin to read this, it should already be clear that humans use paper for a wide range of everyday items. Paper in various forms is an integral part of education, recreation, shipping, and human culture as a whole. In fact, paper as we know it has deep roots running back to China around the year 100. Paper's importance in the ancient world cannot be overstated, as it allowed for the collection and spread of information throughout the world. For a very long time paper was an incredibly valuable item, with the pride of many ancient cultures being large libraries filled with different texts. Paper today is a far cry from the sheets refined by a Chinese court official almost two thousand years ago, however.

Early humans used a wide variety of writing implements before we were able to harness the ability to make true paper. Ancient cultures wrote down and stored knowledge by writing on stones, bones, animal skins, and bark. The Egyptians of antiquity made heavy use of scrolls created from strips of papyrus pounded into each other until they formed a cohesive sheet. Papyrus was quickly degraded through time and other environmental wears, however. At around the same time the Maya were writing on sheets of amate, made by soaking bark in water, filtering out fibers, and then pressing them into a single sheet. Amate is believed to be the very beginnings of true paper. The process of breaking down materials into individual fibers and then pressing them into a thin layer is still used today. This allows for the creation of smooth, uniform sheets rather than the rough and uneven surfaces of other writing implements. Ancient bark amate was still a very rough and uneven paper, however, and it took the Chinese to figure out that a mixture of different ingredients worked well at making more suitable sheets.

    The first paper used in ancient China was a fragile rice paper. In need of more resiliency and inspired by the paper mache nests of wasps, a mixture of hemp, mulberry wood, old fishing nets, and cloth rags was soaked and heated until it turned into a pulpy mass of fibers. Once formed into a sheet, the resulting mix worked very well at creating a smooth and flat piece of paper. The first recorded use for this paper was to protect mirrors as they were transported, however it quickly caught on that it could be used for writing as well. This new style of paper quickly spread to the Middle East, where the first known paper mills were created. As word of this incredibly useful material spread throughout the world, many cultures started boiling rags as a main source of paper fiber; especially in the Middle East and Europe, whole paper industries relied on so-called 'rag pickers' to bring in scraps of clothing to then be rendered into pulp. In early America, colonists relied heavily on hemp as a source of paper fiber. Although more costly to produce, paper made from hemp is much stronger than traditional wood paper. In fact, the first two drafts of the Declaration of Independence were written on durable hemp paper. Plants like hemp produce fiber much faster than trees do, and luckily a pilot program for growing industrial hemp has been active in North Carolina since 2015. If it works out well, we may see the state become one of the first to begin reusing this prolific resource.

    While the processes used to make the perfect paper are still constantly changing, the secret ingredient of our modern paper is wood pulp. In the mid-1800s a process was discovered that allowed for paper to be made using tree fibers. Since then, the vast majority of our paper has come from wood. By using either mechanical or chemical processes, America alone turns over 60 million trees a year into paper. Most of these trees come from carefully managed logging sites, however there are also companies based on recycling used paper and turning it into other materials. With demand for paper growing at a constant and staggering pace, we will need to focus on other sustainable practices for making paper as we continue scribbling into the future.

Natural Dyes

Dyes have been a part of human life for millennia. It didn't take long for people to realize that some of the incredible colors in nature could be transferred to textiles. Across multiple cultures it's been a tradition as old as history itself to throw literally anything nearby into a pot to try and make a dye. The ingredients of these dyes varied wildly depending on location. For example, a majority of reds in ancient India were created using plant roots, while Maya clothiers relied on crushed scale bugs to achieve a scarlet hue. Dyes were considered extremely valuable during ancient times. Roman citizens collected countless sea snails by hand in order to make the perfect purple. Across the globe, ancient Chinese dynasties perfected the art of cultivating silkworms and feeding them specific diets in order to create even more materials to dye. In some ancient cultures dye was worth more than gold. Although large scale dye industries based on natural sources eventually became quite destructive to the environment, today many textiles are colored using synthetic dyes created in laboratories. While we still live in a world dominated by dyes, some of the appreciation for natural dyes has been forgotten since the major introduction of synthetic dyes in the 1850s. This growing season, I encourage you to reconnect with one of our most ancient traditions as a species by trying to dye something. It might be easier than you think.

Many modern dyes utilize chemical reactions in order to bind colors to fabric. This makes the dye long lasting, incredibly precise, and relatively quick to use, however some of these chemicals are harmful to the environment when spilled or released haphazardly. Natural dyes, on the other hand, can sometimes have varied results with unexpected and impressive outcomes. While there are some natural dyes strong enough to dye fabric on their own, many require the aid of other ingredients to help them stick. The dying process is relatively simple but usually involves boiling ingredients in a pot and adding whatever you'd like dyed.

Using plants is a great way to make a dye—if you've ever fallen onto the grass while wearing lightly colored pants you might be familiar with the staining potential of plants. There are some pretty interesting North American native plants that can be used to make dyes. Bloodroot (red), pokeweed (purple), blue wild indigo (blue), sumac (red-yellow), alder (tan-red), and black walnut (black-brown) were used extensively as dyes by early Americans. Goldenrod (yellow), red maple (red), honey locust (tan-green), marigolds (yellow), and stinging nettle (gray-green) are also all commonly found dye makers. The cheeky smartweed (pink) can be used to make a dye as well. After you've used jewelweed as a quick remedy for poison ivy, you can use it to dye your clothes yellow to orange. Speaking of poison ivy, don't get it confused with the lovely native Virginia creeper. This vine can make a pinkish dye, which isn't surprising if you've ever seen its brilliant fall color. Some lichen that grow on rocks or trees can also be used to make dyes. There are even mushrooms that can produce staining pigments.

If you are less outdoor inclined, you can still experiment with natural dyes. Picking up some natural dye producers can be as easy as taking a trip to the supermarket. Spinach (green), beets (pink-red), and blueberries (pink) can be used to dye things. If you eat a good deal of avocados, save the pits and skins. They actually make a subtle red dye. If you are going to collect plants from the wild, be responsible and act sustainably. Please only take what you need and only collect in legal areas.

The History of Glass

The first American glass factory was established in Virginia in the early 1600s, however glass crafting has been a part of human industry and culture since long before that time. This was not only a local craft—humans have worked closely with glass for thousands of years. Glass has helped us throughout history by shaping the way we made tools, stored items, and furnished our houses. Humans first discovered and manipulated glass that naturally formed, however as our cultures advanced we have learned to tame this translucent anomaly.

Simply put, glass occurs when crystalline sand and/or rocks melt into a liquid form and are then very rapidly cooled. When melted, the original crystalline structure is thrown into disarray. By rapidly cooling this molten mixture, the chaotic atomic structure is frozen in place without the chance to re-form a crystalline structure. This gives glass unique properties compared to its original crystalline form, such as a microscopically smooth surface and the ability to transmit, refract, and reflect light effectively. The process of heating crystalline materials followed by almost instant cooling can be achieved through a variety of ways.

Glass is formed naturally through relatively violent events. Lightning strikes in a desert can create twisted columns made up of glass and other materials called fulgurites. Meteorite impacts are thought to have caused other rare types of natural glass known as tektites. Moldavite is a popular form of glass thought to have been formed through such a cosmic collision. The same can be said for Libyan desert glass, a beautiful example of which is found on the chest ornament buried with

Tutankhamun. Ancient human cultures also made use of natural glass formed through volcanic eruptions, known as obsidian, and fashioned it into blades sharper than steel scalpels. Obsidian is found only where a lava flow meets the ocean.

It took humans thousands of years to figure out how to make glass. The first signs of a true glass industry arise around the time of ancient Egypt. After the invention of glass blowing in Syria, the ancient Romans experimented heavily in the art of glass making. As technologies allowed for greater amounts of glass to be made in high quality, its advantages for use as a container and building material began to take hold. Much like the origins of textile dying, artisans soon realized that by adding different materials together their glass would take on different colors and properties. Ancient recipes have been found to include everyday ingredients such as plant materials and ritual sacrifice.

Modern-day glass takes on a multitude of forms and attributes depending on the mix of materials used to make it. The majority of glass is made of mostly silica or silicon dioxide, also known as quartz. Quartz is mixed with a wide variety of ingredients depending on the final product desired. Exciting new developments in glass are still taking place today. An example is electrochromic glass, which has a complex series of layers that respond to electric signals. This has led to windows that are able to become opaque or clear at the flick of a switch. Fiber optics also utilize long strands of glass in order to transmit extremely fast and efficient signals using light. These and other incredible advancements in glass technology will undoubtedly ensure that glass and humans stay closely connected for a very long time.

A Lick of Salt

Salts, combinations of elements that form crystalline structures when close together and dissolve in water and other solvents, are some of the most important compounds on Earth. There are many different kinds of salts depending on the elements that are used in their construction, and advances in the way we understand the way salts form and reform their ordered structures have led to technologies such as lithium batteries, pharmaceuticals, and even nuclear reactors. Most life on Earth, and humanity in particular, is closely tied to a specific form of salt found commonly in our oceans. Referred to as table salt, salt, or halide, sodium chloride is a salt consisting of sodium and chloride ions. Sodium chloride has been used by living beings on Earth since they first began to take shape. Countless organisms have relied on salt in order to regulate nerve impulses, control the flow of fluids, and change their pH. Humans are no different in this regard, and since we lose salt through perspiration it is a requirement for a healthy diet. While some of the food we eat naturally contains salt, its necessity, usefulness, and enchanting taste has led to salt becoming one of the natural compounds that many people are the most familiar with using.

Salt can be harvested through living or buried oceans. Seawater contains around 3.5% salt, and entire ancient cultures were built around placing seawater in large shallow vats. These vats were then either boiled or allowed to sit in the sun in order to evaporate as much water as possible, leaving precious salt behind. The salt was then used primarily to preserve food by drawing out excess moisture and killing any bacteria trying to take hold. Ancient people relied on the dehydrating power of sea salt in order to travel long distances without worrying about spoiled food. Unfortunately, new research is showing that most of the sea salt currently on the market contains tiny pieces of plastic due to plastic pollution. It is still unclear what effects these pieces will have on the long-term health of consumers.

Oceans that were active millennia ago but have long since dried up left behind huge salt deposits buried hundreds of feet underground. These underground deposits are where most of the pure white and finely grained table salt we frequently use comes from. This ancient salt is heavily refined to remove impurities, which depending on the mine's location can give the salt various colors and mineral contents. The difficulty in obtaining salt through evaporation or mining made it incredibly valuable to the ancient world. While we are quite used to it, the amount of salt the average household keeps on hand in order to flavor food is quite literally equal to a medieval king's share. Interestingly, only a small fraction of the salt that we use goes towards food. Most of the salt currently consumed is used in the chemical industry and on frozen winter roads.

While plants rely on various salts in order to function correctly, they do not have an efficient way of disposing of excess salt. Instead of simply sweating it out, plants usually sequester surplus salt into leaves that they then jettison from the plant. This means that when plants are exposed to high levels of salt, such as when roads are salted in the winter time leading to salt-heavy runoff, they tend to drop a lot of leaves at the very least. Resist the temptation to bury your property in a layer of salt this winter and only use it as a last resort, relying instead on sand to provide most of the necessary traction in heavily trafficked areas if possible.

Bricks

When we look at life in the ancient world, we can often identify fundamental forms of items and materials that are still in use today. A successful archaeological dig might yield cutlery, weapons, writing utensils, and clothing that bear a striking resemblance to modern commodities. Most of the items, inventions, and attires that survive from ancient cultures have been used and changed so significantly throughout time that their original forms were quite different than what they are today, however. All around us, there is one inheritance from the ancient world that is still relatively unchanged from its roots in antiquity and is quite literally holding up the foundations of this country. I'm talking about our friend the humble clay brick.

Bricks were first made by ancient cultures needing an alternative to stone or wood for the construction of houses and roads. This first began an estimated 10,000 years ago in the area around modern-day Iraq, where transporting stone and other heavy materials over large distances was difficult or impossible. These first bricks were simple mixes of clay and straw that were allowed to dry in the sun, slathered with mud, and stuck together. The first bricks slowly degraded when exposed to the elements and were in need of quick improvement. The rise and fall of entire civilizations at this time depended on perfecting the durability and manufacture of bricks. Many large cities were located in areas that were rich in the clays and other ingredients needed for bricks. Over time, developments by the ancient Egyptians, Romans, and Chinese dynasties led to the kiln-fired clay bricks that we use today. The romans loved bricks so much that they used legions of workers to distribute bricks all over Europe using portable kilns. While many aspects of day to day life have changed for humans over the years, bricks are very much still in style. There are over 7 billion bricks made each year—that's almost enough to make two great walls of China! There are many reasons why bricks have been able to stick around for so long—and it's more than the mortar.

The first and foremost reason is convenience. During times where the transport of heavy building materials was difficult, some areas had the ability to create materials from the surrounding landscape. This was shown to great effect when building the Biltmore estate outside of Asheville NC, where a brick factory was built on-site to create the 11 million bricks that ended up going into creating the structure. Incredibly, that's more than the 10 million in the Empire State Building. Kiln-fired bricks also resist the elements incredibly well and are proven insulators. They retain a good deal of fire resistance, making them great in cities or other fire-prone areas. Bricks are interesting to look at as well. The various colors from bricks depend on the mineral content of the clay used. The typical red color comes from iron oxide. This bright red hue was the reason that industrial era London allegedly mandated new buildings be built of brick—in the hopes that they would be easier to see and avoid by fog choked motorists.

North Carolina is home to a large amount of clay. In fact, the state prides itself on containing a good deal of a soil type known as Cecil soil, which is especially great for crops and contains a critical amount of certain clay types. This abundance of clay is one of the reasons that there is such a large brick industry in the state—North Carolina is the second highest producer of bricks in the United States. The next time you're out and about, take a moment to admire a brick along your path. Due to generations of artisans utilizing clay and honing the art of brickmaking, chances are it will be around longer than any of us!

Mulch Matters

Mulch is a word synonymous with proper landscaping techniques, and for good reason. Large areas of bare soil in between plantings tend to dry out quickly, erode in heavy rainfalls, and attract weeds surprisingly fast. While a landscape benefits from small areas of bare soil or sparse mulch in order to attract beneficial wildlife, mulch 2-3 inches deep spread across landscape and garden beds works wonders at keeping soil temperatures at reasonable levels, preserving moisture, halting the germination of weed seeds, and in many cases enriching the soil beneath it. The general definition of mulch is any material that serves to give bare areas of soil a shield against environmental and weed pressures while still allowing water, air, and organisms to reach the ground beneath. Wood chips, leaves, grass, stones, and rubber are among the many things that are used for this purpose. While many aspects of a landscape are fluid depending on the aesthetic or engineering tastes of the owner, when it comes to mulch there are clear winners and losers on which type to use.

First and foremost, keep your rubber on the road and out of the landscape. While it outlasts some other choices, rubber smells awful and leeches mysterious substances into the ground around it. For an attractive and long-lasting solution, stone can be a good choice, especially in high traffic areas. Bark nuggets are large clumps of bark that can be used as a heavy, low maintenance mulch as well. Some gardeners use landscape fabric under stones and other heavy mulches, however I encourage you to resist the urge as these tightly woven layers actually prevent water and ground nesting beneficial organisms from having proper access to the soil. While stones and other long-lasting mulches require minimal maintenance to look their best, quickly decomposing mulches like leaves and wood chips are the masters of the mulch kingdom. Properly applied, these mulches provide adequate protection to the soil while at the same time also being permeable enough to allow wildlife and plant essentials through. Although these mulches usually have to be reapplied multiple times per year, they are not leaving your beds. As organic mulches break down, their nutrients are incorporated into the soil around them. They also harbor populations of beneficial fungi and bacteria which help your plants with nutrient absorption.

    Wood chips are usually available aged or 'fresh'. Use aged for most garden and landscape beds as this will readily break down and benefit the plants around it. Wood chips that are not aged break down slower and are more practical for beds out of the way and hard to reach for repeated applications. Another good choice is leaves, although they decompose rapidly and require the most frequent re-ups. Avoid using leaves from walnut trees for mulch as they can inhibit plant growth. Leaf mulch can be bought or made yourself from the refuse that falls and floats to the ground throughout the year. Pine needles are a good alternative to leaves if you have a good source, and are especially helpful to use on slopes as they tend to resist being swept away by water more than other kinds of mulch.

    Whatever type of mulch you choose, keeping layers of 2-3 inches in your garden beds will help you spend less time weeding and watering your landscapes. Avoid piling mulch in contact with the base of plants as this can lead to fungal build-ups or other problems. Mulch layers do not need to be universally thick, however. Leaving small areas of sparse or absent mulch wherever possible, usually towards the edges of your property and behind plants, is extremely useful as this gives the thousands of beneficial soil-dwelling garden denizens a place to easily settle down and be of benefit to you and your landscapes.

Our Water Supply

Most are familiar with the water cycle—the process through which water in surface collections like lakes and oceans evaporates and rises to become clouds, which can travel long distances before raining down on another part of the planet. The water cycle ensures that water is transported inland and supplies fresh water essential to most life. Huge amounts of water are shed during each thunderstorm. On average, a storm that rains an inch of water pours over 25,000 gallons per acre of land. Some of this water immediately flows on the surface towards streams, rivers, or other bodies of water. On the other hand, a good deal of rain turns into groundwater. This is when water seeps down through the soil until it reaches porous subsurface rocks and collects at a depth known as the water table.

To give you an idea of how deep this normally is, the water table in and around Western NC averages around 30-40 feet below the surface, however this can vary considerably depending on location and even the time of year. In some areas, the water table is mere inches from the surface. Large collections of water in porous rock, known as aquifers, are a major source for drinking water in the rural U.S. and provide water for up to 40% of the global population. Most of the freshwater on the planet is tucked away in the cracks and crevices of the planet's crust—more than 95% of the available (non-frozen) freshwater on Earth is groundwater. This incredibly important resource less than four stories below our feet is filtered by rocks and soil as it percolates down to the water table. We must remain vigilant to protect it, however, as groundwater is shockingly easy to pollute by both natural and human means.

Humans unfortunately play a large role in groundwater pollution. Oil and gasoline from roads and driveways flow into rivers and seep into groundwater. Aging septic systems seep sewage into the soil (say that three times fast), leading to deadly bacteria buildups. Batteries can leak acids if disposed of improperly. In general, anything that seeps into the ground can get into the groundwater. Some pesticides take a long time to break down, and can be found in the soil and groundwater for years after an application. Once present in the water table pesticides can be exposed to other organisms outside of the intended treatment zone. Pesticides also collect in runoff, which by travelling through an area can combine to form a deadly cocktail upon entering a nearby stream, river, or lake. This can drastically affect aquatic animals which tend to be extra susceptible to these chemicals. Once in the water these pesticides are extremely difficult to remove; an unsettling report in early 2019 also found that neonicotinoids, a common class of pesticide, can actually become more harmful to humans during normal water treatment processes such as chlorination and alkaline hydrolysis.

Many of the watersheds in America consist of protected forest environments, like much of the Appalachian region, leading to largely pristine water stores. This does not mean the water is pure, however—groundwater naturally takes on different properties depending on the subsurface rocks present. Some aquifers in the Asheville, NC area are known to contain elevated amounts of naturally occurring iron, for example. Many of these natural contaminants are fine for your health, however to get an idea of what is in your drinking water, I recommend getting it tested regularly if you draw water from a private well. Wells access water directly from the water table, so water that seeps into the ground around your well is a large part of what you are drinking. Keep in mind that as water percolates through the soil it could also be picking up contaminants. As recent events with industrial pollutants like coal ash have shown, homeowners cannot count on local governments or businesses alone to test the drinking water in their area. Visit https://www.groundwater.org/get-informed/basics/testing.html to learn more about how to test your well water.

The Dangers Saturating Our World

We live in a world dominated by conveniences. Throughout human history, countless inventions have been manufactured in the search for an easier life. Our food and water remain chilled mere steps from the TV, artificial light beams throughout the night, and our primary modes of transportation are powerful, quiet, and efficient. The list goes on and on, however one of the most glaring ways in which humans have tried to simplify our day-to-day lives is our production of pesticides. Renewed attention around the effects of these pesticides on the world's plant and animal life has made it clear that the long-term effects of exposure are poorly understood at best. It can be easy to forget that these chemicals are affecting humans as well.

A pesticide is basically anything that is used to kill pests. As humans became more adept at farming, farms growing the same or similar plants together in large collections became widespread. Tracts of land devoted to a single crop, called monocultures, are magnets for pests and diseases since they basically form a giant buffet for any interested parties. This led to a wide variety of insecticides and herbicides being used in fields in order to keep these pests and diseases to a manageable level. Ancient cultures used natural methods of pest control such as dusting with sulfur and companion plantings, however as we moved into the industrial revolution people discovered that some of the new synthetic chemicals being mixed up were pretty good at killing crop pests as well.

The rising use of monocultures as the preferred way of farming combined with eager chemists looking to solve the associated pest problems eventually led to the 'spray and forget' culture surrounding pesticides that we have today. It is estimated that an incredible 2.5 million tons of pesticides are sprayed every year, the majority of which are herbicides designed to kill weeds. Much of this is sprayed by individual homeowners looking for a quick and easy way to tidy up their property. Studies are beginning to show that these pesticides might be having some pretty profound impacts on the environment and as a consequence humans as well.

One of the most impressive and terrifying aspects of many pesticides is their ability to persist in an environment long after their original application. This makes it very easy to come into contact with a pesticide. Every trip to the store, family night out, and sleepy Saturday morning at home is laced with a multitude of exposures to various poisons. The human body is equipped with powerful abilities to render many harmful substances inert, however studies have shown that some synthetic chemicals actually build up in our systems slowly over time. Many of these chemicals are the same things that are commonly used in farms, gardens, and households worldwide. While I hate to be a downer, there have been some important recent studies performed that give insight into how truly saturated in pesticides our world really is. It is our responsibility to keep up to date on this topic so that we can readily make changes as they become necessary.

Most pesticide peddlers work very hard at downplaying the true nature of their poisons through bright, attractive labels and catchy product names. It works. I remember having hands drenched in Round-Up as a child while I performed my weekly chores. While exposure such as this is not outright deadly, repeated exposures to pesticides have been shown to lead to large accumulations of chemicals in the body. Some of these chemicals have immediate negative effects. Glyphosate, the main active ingredient in Round-Up, has been found to severely disrupt the gut bacteria in honey bees for example. It would be practical to assume that humans are similarly affected in some way. Many pesticides are filtered through the liver which in the long term accumulates wear and tear through this constant work. What isn't filtered out becomes stored in fat cells, sometimes reacting with other chemicals in the body and turning into more harmful forms.

Even though the winter months reduce pesticide exposure through outside forces, many common household items can be riddled with hazards. A cursory daydream about government-owned health watchdog organizations usually conjures up images of buildings filled with an endless stream of faceless scientists and unlimited funding aimed at rigorously testing every chemical and product that comes onto the market. While the methodology is there, unfortunately many of these bodies lack the manpower and funding to truly protect our citizens or our environment. This leads to high levels of pesticides, all of which have unknown long-term effects on humans and the ecosystem, being present in a startling variety of items.

This is not necessarily due to any negligence or malice, however. The frightening truth is that many of these chemicals have only been in use for a short amount of time, and we are just now beginning to see some of the unintended effects that they are having beyond their targets. According to scientists over 90% of pesticides come into contact with organisms other than their intended targets. Some pesticides linger in the soil and water for years at a time, affecting anything unlucky enough to pass through. Systemic insecticides are incorporated into plants and are even found in nectar and pollen, where they kill or damage the brains of pollinators or other animals feeding from them. Some pesticides have been directly or indirectly linked to cancer in humans while others are being shown to inhibit brain development in species such as frogs. In short, it seems we know far less about the long-term effects of pesticide use than we would like to think.

Interestingly enough, intense public outcry in the states over ecological damage from pesticides was not spurred by the government bodies whose only job is to ensure the safety of American lands and people. Instead, it wasn't until Rachel Carson published her book Silent Spring in 1962 that some of the deeply rooted consequences of widespread pesticide use became well known to the public. This helped lead to the ban of the compound DDT, a pesticide widely used from the 40s up until the 70s and which was found to have devastating negative effects on the environment. Time will tell us the true effects of more recent commonly used pesticides. If we all maintain a responsible discipline over what we disperse into the world around us, and only use pesticides when absolutely necessary and in strict accordance to their labels, we can go a long way in helping to restore some of what we have unwittingly disrupted and in effect ensure the continued survival of the Earth as we know it. In many situations it would be best to find ways to avoid pesticide use altogether. With new data constantly emerging on the effects that pesticides have on plants, people, and wildlife, governments all over the world are beginning to take action at reducing the use or outright banning some of the most widely used pesticides. While pesticides can have their place in preventing disease and pest outbreaks, we should view these powerful chemicals as the very last resort rather than everyday items. We may also need to look how our own farming practices, like monocultures, led to our need to use pesticides in the first place.

As we become more aware of the persistence of pesticides in the world around us, we can take steps to at least reduce the amount we introduce into our systems. In some parts of the country, water companies are able to avoid reporting high pesticide levels due to lax EPA regulations. Recent studies found glyphosate in every sample of Cheerios and Quaker Oats that were tested. Tea leaves are found pleasant to a wide variety of animals, which usually necessitates high levels of pesticides during the growing season. This has led to many large-scale tea brands selling tea with high amounts of pesticides still on the leaves. Some companies even treat their individual paper bags with toxins. If you or your family consumes these items, do some research into alternate brands. While modern agriculture has worked itself into a corner where frequent pesticide use is almost unavoidable, it is time that homeowners think more than twice about using them in the future.

Insect Decline

Insects are in many ways the driving forces behind the ecosystems that we depend on for food, oxygen, soil health, and more. Evolutionarily speaking they are some of the oldest animals on the planet, and are intricately intertwined with basically every aspect of the environment. While there are currently around 900 thousand insect species known to science, most scientists agree that there are many, many more insect species yet to be formally discovered. This makes insects the most varied group of animals by far. There is also a huge amount of them—an estimated 10 quintillion insects are alive at any one time (10 followed by 18 zeros). Most of these insects are tiny and live among the soil, however there are so many insects that an insect is specialized at filling pretty much every role in an ecosystem. With impressive stats like these, it is easy to see that insects are a critical part of the natural world around us. Unfortunately, scientists have noticed alarming trends in recent years that point to many of these insects suffering drastic population declines over the last few decades. Let's take a look at some of these findings, and the impacts that a drastic loss of insects could have on the world as a whole.

Media attention was focused on insect decline when a study was published in 2017 showing that in protected areas dotting German agricultural zones, the biomass (overall weight) of all flying insects decreased by up to 82% over the previous 27 years. Other similar studies have shown a decline in abundance for over half of monitored populations. There have been few long term studies like these in the U.S., however it can be assumed that we are suffering similar declines. While these statistics are staggering, the German study in particular was focused on isolated untamed areas in between farms. These are probably some of the areas with the fewest active wildlife populations due to fragmented habitats, sparse and inconsistent food, and high pesticide use in the surrounding areas. Hopefully many areas don't share the same devastating amount of insect loss. One of the most pressing problems of this issue is actually tying down a direct cause so that we can begin working towards a solution. The current insect decline seems to be propelled by a multitude of factors including climate change, pollution, increasing highway traffic, artificial light at night, pesticides, habitat loss, and possibly others. While the root causes are still largely unknown, the effects that this might end up having on the environment could be long lasting if not averted.

Insects are relied on by countless organisms for everyday survival. They are eaten by a wide variety of creatures, while at the same time recycling nutrients and materials back into the soil. Many plants have closely linked relationships with insects who help them with pollination, seed dispersal, and defense from pests. This is especially true in the flowering plants, which make up over 90% of all known vascular plant species. Not only do flowering plants and insects mutually benefit from the process of pollination, it is believed that insect/plant interactions in ancient times might have been what caused flowering plants to begin their unique evolutionary paths to begin with. While many ecosystems are capable of adapting to catastrophic changes, the wide variety of roles that insects fill means that even a small reduction in their numbers would be incredibly impactful.

It is critical that we pay close attention to the loss of insects in an effort to understand not only the underlying reasons but also the ripple effects that can then resonate throughout ecosystems as a whole. The longer we sit by and let these creatures disappear, the more priceless resources are lost right under our noses. As we work to better understand the complex workings of insects in our environment, perhaps the most important lesson to take from the current focus on insect declines is that we still know very little about how and why these animals operate.

Chapter Six

A LOOK TO THE FUTURE

Rising CO_2 Levels Have Far Reaching Effects on Plants

There's a lot of talk going on right now about rising carbon dioxide (CO_2) levels in the atmosphere and what that means. While there may be a debate on the main causes of this recent rise, we are experiencing the highest concentration of carbon dioxide in our environment ever seen by humankind. Spikes such as this have happened somewhat frequently in the history of the Earth, however many scientists are concerned about this recent increase in part because it has happened extremely fast and is beginning to impact plants in ways we did not expect. This is not a piece discussing the causes of rising CO_2 in the atmosphere. Instead, let's look at the impact that it is already having on our environment and economy so that we can better understand the problem we are dealing with.

Carbon dioxide is an important element of our atmosphere. It helps regulate the temperature of the planet and it serves as an integral part of photosynthesis, the process by which plants produce energy. The amount of carbon dioxide in our atmosphere has generally fluctuated throughout history, rising and falling due to changes in climate and the types of dominant organisms. Current levels are much higher than what we have found in samples of ancient ice dating back up to 800,000 years. Since plants rely on CO_2 to grow, one would think that with higher concentrations of CO_2 in the environment, plants might be able to reach gargantuan sizes at record speeds due to CO_2 being more readily available to use for photosynthesis. This is indeed what is happening. Plants are growing at a faster rate than before, and they are able to produce more stored energy in the form of sugars, starches, and fats. While this might sound great on paper, it is having some potentially devastating side effects as well.

Even though plants are growing faster than before, research is beginning to show that the food being produced by them is actually less nutritious than before as well. Because plants are able to produce an increased amount of stored energy, this excess is serving to crowd out other nutrients such as zinc, potassium, iron, and calcium from plants. This leads to crops that have less nutrients and protein. In addition to this, research is starting to show that the additional increase in temperature due to increased CO_2 negatively impacts global crop yields at the staggering rate of between 3.5 to 8.5 billion dollars for every additional ton of CO_2 emitted. While a ton of CO_2 is a lot of gas, it pales in comparison to the 37.1 billion tons estimated to have been emitted in 2018.

Pollen has been affected by the change in carbon dioxide as well. A recent study by Purdue University has shown that the protein content in goldenrod pollen has dropped by a third since the 1800s. This is very impactful to pollinators, especially bees that have evolved to feed their young specific amounts of pollen. It is unclear how a protein-deficient diet will affect these species, however shorter life spans should be expected which could lead to pollination difficulties. The rise of CO_2 concentrations has also started to change leaves. Normally plants use tiny openings in their leaves to inhale CO_2 and exhale water. Plants are starting to develop leaves with fewer of these openings since carbon dioxide is easier to grab in the air, while as a consequence they might start releasing less water back into the atmosphere.

Forests are a large consumer of CO_2 in the atmosphere, however some scientists are concerned that due to rising global temperatures and drier summers these plants will be unable to grow as fast as possible. This would make forests less effective at absorbing carbon dioxide than they normally are. Several industrious companies have taken this opportunity to step up and try to fill this gap in global CO_2 absorption.

For example, a small European firm is hoping to make use of giant fans and special materials that act like CO_2 sponges in order to siphon CO_2 from the air and utilize it for purposes such as greenhouse growing or soda bottling. Unfortunately such CO_2 capture technologies appear to be costly and power-intensive. As they become more refined perhaps they will help in reducing the amount of atmospheric CO_2. The soil itself is home to a decent amount of carbon dioxide, due to the fact that some micro-organisms sequester CO_2 into specially designed proteins tucked away in any available nooks and crannies. A significant amount of CO_2 finds its way into the oceans as well.

It is believed that around 25% of carbon dioxide emissions end up in the ocean. Millions of tons of CO_2 are absorbed by the ocean each day. These huge amounts of CO_2 are starting to lead to extreme side effects, as increased carbon dioxide in the oceans make them more acidic. Scientists believe that our oceans are 30% more acidic than they were 200 years ago. This is having some pretty strange impacts on sea life. While some animals, like jellyfish, seem to thrive in waters with higher acidity, others are literally being burned alive by the recent influx. Studies have shown that the shells of some creatures are being eaten away by the increase in acidity, for example. Higher acidity also appears to change the behavior of young fish. Fish raised in environments with high acidity appear to move from the protection of darker waters into dangerous well-lit areas much faster in their development cycle than normal. These fish also seemed to have a slower start in growth rates compared to those raised in waters with low acidity. The frightening truth is that we have little knowledge of the true effects that rising acidity will have on the oceans as a whole.

It is important to keep the impacts of rising atmospheric CO_2 in mind as we take steps to slow the speed of emissions and seek to learn their effects on the world around us. Learn more about your carbon footprint and ways to reduce it by visiting https://www3.epa.gov/carbon-footprint-calculator/.

Helpful Viruses

The fall and winter, seasons of beautiful foliage and blanketing snow, are also the seasons commonly known for the spread of viruses. Punctuated by bouts of the common cold, the flu, and other viruses, this is the time of year that finds a greater incidence of people huddling together inside to get out of the cold which as we all know is perfect for the spread of illness. Although even their name usually evokes negative connotations, viruses are constantly around us and provide more to the environment than making us sick. Viruses are basically tiny parasites hundreds of times smaller than a bacteria cell, however they can still wreak havoc given the right circumstances. It is estimated that in America alone there are around a billion cases of the cold each year. That only accounts for one type of virus-borne illness, and there are thousands more that make their rounds no matter the season. Viruses have perfected ways in which they attach to cells, insert genetic material into those cells, and then reprogram the affected cells in order to make them do what they want. Usually this involves churning out specific proteins that are then packaged into new copies of the virus so that it can continue to spread. Since viruses are so good at getting materials into cells, they are being used in areas such as the medical and agricultural sectors for multiple applications.

Viruses have been intensely studied for over 100 years. By watching how viruses are able to hijack a cell into making specific proteins and then arrange those proteins inside of a protective and mobile structure, scientists have learned some of the secrets behind cellular transport and replication. Studies in the 1920s showed that plants could be protected from devastating viral outbreaks if they were introduced to a weaker strain first. Our flu shots work in a similar way, introducing our immune system to a virus in a harmless state so that it can prepare defenses before a true assault. Viruses have been engineered to perform more active combat roles as well. Scientists have been able to declaw the rabies virus, for example, removing the disease-causing elements and designing viruses that are currently being used to help combat a multitude of disease causing cells. Research is currently being conducted on the use of viruses in order to ward off invasive pests and diseases such as the red fire ant and the bee disease American foulbrood. Viruses have also been repurposed to help introduce specific 'tracker' molecules into cells that help scientists with genetic engineering. Due to their ability to automatically construct themselves into different forms, viruses are being looked at as a method of molecular construction for the future. Some scientists believe that properly altered viruses could form microscopic scaffolds allowing for precise and directed surgical and restorative applications. While mostly theoretical, there are other potential uses for modified viruses as well. According to some, microscopic batteries constructed by viral workers could soon help power the world of tomorrow.

The study of viruses is an exciting and ever-changing area in science today. By looking closely at the lifestyle of viruses we can learn a great deal about how the world works on a microscopic level. While the ability to reprogram viruses to perform important genetic and cellular work is incredibly powerful and impressive, we cannot forget that these are lessons learned from nature and not created wholly by ourselves. The incredible complexity and efficiency that is present in these tiny hijackers deserves a good deal of respect. Appropriate caution must be taken as we create and release these new viral applications into the world as only time will tell their lasting effects on the Earth as a whole.

Plants in Space

'Plants in Space' sounds like it could be the title of an upcoming science fiction blockbuster or a lost David Bowie track, however the study of how plants survive space travel is a bustling field at the moment. Advances in space travel have made it possible to soon begin exploring our solar system using human crews. Growing plants on board space-faring vessels or in established colonies will help us survive these long journeys for a variety of reasons. Having plants growing off-world can help rejuvenate air, supply food, and provide a critical connection to the planet such expeditions leave behind. Extraterrestrial gardens are not as simple as you might think, however. Equipment used for space travel is forced to be as small and light as possible, leading to even the most lavish space plot being able to house only a few plants each grow cycle. At the same time otherworldly forces found in space, like microgravity, act on plants in mysterious ways. As we take to the stars on long and dangerous missions, it is of critical importance that we learn how to also bring other forms of life with us in order to better weather the dangers of the great beyond.

While a current hot topic, the study of how plants are affected by space is not new. In the 40s the U.S. launched some seeds into space and made them the first organisms blasted into orbit. By the end of the 60s we had launched and recovered three research satellites crammed full of a variety of organisms including plants. It was difficult to assess the true impacts of space travel on plants until astronauts were able to care for and directly observe them. This didn't happen until Russian cosmonauts began to grow pea and mustard plants aboard their cramped Salyut space station in the 70s. While most of their plants died, the resident cosmonauts became so attached to the survivors that they were hard pressed to leave their new foliating friends. These first space plants were grown mostly for research purposes. They performed wonders at raising crew morale as well, however, and served as a literal growing reminder of the planet the crew had left behind and that they were working to improve.

Plant studies aboard the various space stations have expanded over the years, with the U.S. beginning major studies in 1999. Plant studies have slowly grown on the space station, which was recently upgraded with its largest ever plant chamber. This fully automated greenhouse is about the size of a large microwave and is equipped with multiple LEDs, sensors, and watering systems. While these tiny space farms give astronauts little room to stretch their green thumbs, the data they are providing is helping scientists figure out the unique obstacles that future astronauts will need to surmount when growing plants in space. Astronauts have been able to sample some of their crops, however it is still difficult to grow enough to sustain even a single crew member. Eventually, growing methods will be fine-tuned enough to allow for reliable food sources on future space voyages. At the same time, these rocket propelled greenhouses will work wonders at recycling the carbon dioxide in the air around them into more human friendly forms. There are several main problems that plants have when it comes to growing off-planet, however. Low or nonexistent gravity, cramped quarters, artificial light, and unique growing methods all serve to affect space plants in a variety of ways.

Small, artificially lit chambers usually lead to small plants which are susceptible to damage in the case of poor air circulation or excess moisture. Artificial lighting can certainly be used to grow plants, however even the most advanced UV bulbs are still eclipsed by normal sunlight in terms of growing power. Soil is often deemed too heavy for transport, and is usually substituted by either baked clay or hydroponic systems. This leads to plants that end up missing out on the benefits that microorganisms in our soil provide, including increased nutrient and water absorption. Many plants have internal mechanisms that also depend on the effects of gravity in order to function properly. Most plants possess specific starch structures in their cells that are able to detect gravity based on how they rise or fall. It is believed that plants use this information to help guide their direction of growth, however astronauts on the space station are currently studying the other methods that plants use to detect the gravity around them. Root and seedling growth seem affected by low gravity in a variety of ways, however scientists are still divining the true effects that low or non-existent gravity could have on long term plant growth. Just as in humans, the effects that living for long periods of time away from Earth's gravity can have on plants are largely unknown, as some of our most important and complex cellular processes utilize the effects of gravity to operate effectively.

Water also acts strangely in low gravity and tends to form sticky globs, requiring the construction of specialized watering mechanisms for plants. Without the protection of the Earth's magnetic field, plants in space will be bombarded by higher levels of radiation than normal. Recently scientists have detected changes in space-raised plant cells such as disrupted carbohydrate storage, wherein the affected cells seem to store accumulations of oils instead of the normal starch. It seems that many of the plants grown in space so far have experienced at least some degree of gene scrambling in the process as well. Even though plants are the perfect solution to help renew air, recycle waste, and provide food for future space travels, there are still many more questions to be answered before we will be able to create any true space oases. While scientists work hard at understanding the true effects that space travel can have on plants, we will perhaps also gain insight into the ways that humans are changed by such otherworldly journeys as well.

Solar Fields and Native Plantings

In 2015, the solar energy produced in North Carolina was enough to power over 200,000 homes. Utility-scale projects make up the majority of this industry, which require huge tracts of land that are made into barren areas virtually unlivable to most wildlife. Some solar companies are beginning to try and change that, however, and one of the best ways to do so is to implement pollinator habitats focused on native plants in the areas surrounding solar panels. This has some pretty incredible benefits to the solar fields themselves as well as the environment.

Solar projects around the world have begun planting native perennial groundcover, mostly wildflowers and meadow grasses, in the spaces underneath and between solar panels. This type of planting is actually an incredibly effective pollinator habitat. While a relatively recent trend, there are some strong benefits to doing so that have already become apparent. Many native plant species such as clover, butterfly weed, and black-eyed susans are extremely resilient in most conditions. They establish strong root systems that help to control stormwater runoff which is a large problem in most solar fields. Interestingly enough, pollinator plantings surrounding solar panels help increase efficiency by helping to keep the panels cool during the day and warm at night. Once established, these wildlife habitats also cut down on maintenance costs by only requiring a quarter of the mowing that turf grass would need. Pollinator habitats in solar farms are clearly cost savers on several levels.

These native plantings also contribute to the surrounding environment in other ways. One of the biggest problems facing our native pollinators is the loss of habitat. In fact, many of our native bees can only forage a few hundred yards away from their nest, making large areas of empty or overdeveloped land uninhabitable. Many of our native species are therefore confined to wild patches in between areas of cultivation or development. Even though these beneficial species are extremely limited in their habitats, they are still able to contribute hundreds of millions of dollars a year to our agriculture industries through pollination alone. Planting native flowers and meadow grasses in solar fields can help in connecting some of these wild areas together, giving wildlife the opportunity to travel to and from areas that were previously inaccessible. This can allow fragmented populations the chance to come together and move throughout their ranges, increasing their genetic diversity and strengthening their ability to fight off environmental stressors.

The overall reason this is so exciting is that large scale industries are starting to shift their views towards conservation wherever possible. Thanks to the steps that ecologically-minded farmers all over the world have already taken in their own operations, we have started to see some of the benefits that a properly functioning ecosystem can bring to our lives and wallets. To use an overwrought cliche, a healthy ecosystem is a well-oiled machine that requires very little outside influence in order to function properly. Solar field pollinator habitats take a step in repairing habitats lost through urbanization and help to repair the functionality of the blooming and buzzing world around us. This relationship is not one sided, however. Recent research by the Department of Energy concluded that if current solar projects switched to pollinator-friendly plantings surrounding solar panels, the surrounding agricultural fields could potentially benefit from millions of dollars of increased crop value simply by being nearby.

As solar sites planted with native plants flourish, hopefully more developers will catch on and design their own sites in similar ways. Minnesota is currently taking the largest strides toward making the plantings around their solar industries native plant focused, instead of using turf grass or bare soil. The solar industry in North Carolina and many other states is already flourishing and presents the opportunity for these states to make a name for themselves as leaders in forward environmental thinking. As far as land development goes, establishing an area that generates power while at the same time providing habitat for valuable native species is a win-win in my opinion.

Epilogue

GARDENS AS ZOOS

The wonders in this book are but a tiny fraction of the miracles performed by the environments around us. Many of these things, and countless others, are unfortunately in danger of being lost forever. While nature flourishes because of change, human impact on the Earth has reached levels that are clearly unsustainable. Through our brilliance and lack of foresight we have succeeded in altering every single aspect of our world, from the vegetables we eat to the animals we encounter. Even our own bodies have been manipulated over generations due to contact with pollutants and synthetic chemicals. It is difficult to truly consider that even with the best intentions, as a species we excel at disruption. In our never-ending struggle to achieve an easier existence we have wrought incredible damage on the natural world that we rely on for food, water, and air. By overestimating the talents and wisdom of ourselves we have altered the Earth in ways that we still poorly understand at best. Humans in the near and distant future will be taught about the crossroads in which we currently stand, one of the largest problems yet faced by our species. The very methods that have brought our species to this golden age of technology also threaten to deeply disturb the future of life on this planet. This was not all done on purpose, of course—it is only through recent advances in the scientific community that we have been able to discern the true effects of applications that were long assumed harmless. However we can no longer hide behind the velvet robe of ignorance. There is still time to heal these wounds. And luckily for us, the framework for our salvation is already growing all around us.

Human intervention in the natural world, while dramatic and long-lasting, is not all bad. An interesting example of this is the development of zoos. While there are many problems involved in housing wild animals in man-made enclosures such as determining proper diets, allowing animals sufficient space, keeping the animals' intellects occupied as to not encourage malaise, and so on, the overall effect that zoos have on the visiting public is a positive one. Zoo patrons usually leave with increased feelings of awe, understanding, and connectedness with the animals they have seen. Some also use the experience to make a connection between the uncontrolled beauty of the natural world and the ways that humans as a whole can disrupt that environment. These lessons are incredibly important—admiration and respect for all living things are the first steps towards actively working to preserve them. Therefore, zoos as a cultural institution should remain at the forefront of education even as we work to make them more comfortable for their occupants. In this direction, there is much work to be done, as unfortunately the true elegance of the animals within is not able to be observed in zoos.

Many natural subtleties are impossible to recreate in a zoo setting—the countless interactions between an animal and its environment shape its physical and mental state into a unique blend of traits that become disjointed once removed from their natural home. We can admire the powerful and vibrant beak of the toucan, and gasp in shock at the beautiful colorations of poison dart frogs, however these observations do little justice to the fine-tuned and meticulously balanced adaptations that these creatures possess. To truly understand how and why animals are made the way they are, they must be observed in their natural habitats. It is only there that we can clearly see how exactly they fit into the puzzle of their individual niches. Although zoos are necessary tools in the education of the natural world, we cannot lose sight of the fact that they are a somewhat flawed means to an end—to enlighten visitors on the wondrous and imperiled world around us. Protecting and restoring natural landscapes, the only areas which allow nature to play its practiced parts, is a no-brainer once love for the creatures who live there has been established. You don't have to travel to your nearest city zoo to make these close connections, however. In fact most of us have zoos in our very own backyards.

While they may be host to a flurry of activity throughout the growing season, many of our gardens exist in a very similar fashion to zoos. In order to retain sanity in this loud and crowded world, it is an uncomfortable fact that we make countless assumptions throughout our lives. We assume that the power will be on, that our cars will operate with little input, and that our governments will work towards our best interests. This is also true in our gardens. We assume for example that since we see insects in gardens that they are healthy and easily accessible ecosystems, when in reality these flying and crawling populations are often fragmented and weakened groups struggling for survival among alien surroundings. Indeed the insects in many of our gardens are a testament to their incredible resilience rather than our skills at fostering them through our plantings. Just like zoos, many gardens are environments far removed from their natural settings. The animals who reside in and around them many times find themselves in unfamiliar territory. As more and more natural ecosystems are transformed into urban landscapes, the overwhelming trend is to plant showy ornamental plants in place of the original occupants. Many of these plants come from exotic locations far removed from the planting site. This has been shown to have devastating effects on local wildlife. Insects are especially impacted by changes in plant types, as many species have maintained close relationships with specific plants over hundreds of millions of years.

As plants and animals have evolved side by side over time, a constant battle has taken place between the two. Eager to ward off unwanted grazers, many plants have developed complex and unique chemical cocktails that are distributed throughout their whole. Many of these chemicals serve to make the plant either unpalatable or downright poisonous. Not to be easily outdone, hungry herbivores slowly developed resistances to these chemicals in order to continue their feasts. This back and forth eventually forged close bonds between these plants and animals, sometimes even leading to symbiotic relationships. Some species are so intertwined with their chosen plants that survival without them is simply not possible. Many butterflies, for example, have developed specific plants on which to rear their offspring. The famous monarch butterfly can only raise its young on a diet of milkweed leaves, as their caterpillars depend on incorporating the milkweed's latex into their own bodies as a way to ward off predators. Most other insects have similarly close relationships with plants. When their preferred plants are removed or become unavailable, these animals have little choice but to leave or die. Even worse still, when a foreign plant is placed into such an environment it can actively harm anything unlucky enough to take a bite. The few insects that are able to stick around are the toughest of the lot, and are usually generalist species that don't depend on any single species to survive. Even while these heavyweights buzz and bound happily around your garden, do not forget that they too have been removed from their environments. Similar to zoos, many of the insects that we see in developed landscapes are only able to utilize a small fraction of their inherited abilities. This leads to extreme population declines in both insects and the animals that depend on them for food.

A recent study by the University of Delaware in conjunction with the Smithsonian Migratory Bird Center highlighted the sobering impact that non-native plant species can have on certain birds. It seems that the less native plants in a landscape, the less likely insectivorous birds like chickadees are able to raise their young. Their research points to the shocking statistic that once the total amount of native plants in a landscape drops below 70% it is unable to support the volume of insects needed to feed growing chickadee families. To a certain extent, the more non-native plants we plant, the more native wildlife we unwittingly exclude from our landscapes. It is therefore important to plant as many native plants in as many places as possible. This can help to restore some of the food, shelter, and nesting sites that have been lost and are sorely needed by a host of animals. Even this idea can spark heated debates between environmentalists, however, as not all of our native plants have survived human contact unchanged.

For as long as we have inhabited this planet, humans have shaped the world to better suit our wants and needs. One of the earliest examples of this is the careful manipulation of plants in order to propagate certain desirable traits. Ancient cultures in central Mexico transformed small tufted grasses into what we now know as corn, and the Romans worked tirelessly to create the perfect rose. Profound changes to these species were wrought through cultivation, wherein the intrepid grower would select plants with certain qualities and breed them together to hopefully ensure offspring with similar traits. This ancient practice still continues to this day, and in fact a large percentage of the plants we eat are specific cultivated varieties—or cultivars—of plants that look very different from their ancestors. Many popular household plant varieties have been designed to dazzle human visitors yet offer very little food, shelter, or nesting sites for wildlife. This can be due to the fact that some cultivars rely on strange mutations in order to accomplish their end goal. Take, for instance, the 'double flower' or 'double bloom' variety seen commonly in roses, lilacs, peonies, and others. Plants of this cultivar are immediately stunning to the eye—their flowers are packed with twice the amount of petals as normal, and seem to almost burst at the seams. This beauty is purely superficial, however, as these added petals are actually mutations of the reproductive structures of the flower itself. This means that while there are larger flowers, any animal visitors looking for nectar or pollen will find their efforts fruitless as little to no pollen is available and the crowd of petals makes nectar collection difficult.

Other plant varieties alter leaf colorations in order to suit the taste of gardeners, but these too can come at a price. Leaf color is usually determined by the chemicals in said leaf, and many of these chemicals also serve to ward off other creatures. Animals reacting with a plant that has altered leaf colors can sometimes come into contact with chemicals that they were not prepared to deal with. In many instances insects are the ones that feel the brunt of these changes, and whole populations are lost when their naturally preferred plants are replaced by poisonous ones overnight. The practice of cultivating specific varieties is not purely for aesthetic purposes, however, and there are many varieties bred in order to be more resilient to environmental stressors. This can make restoring natural landscapes easier in areas that have been deeply disturbed by human development or natural disasters. There are a wide range of cultivated varieties of native plants, sometimes referred to as nativars, that work to solve these problems as well. Some scientists and environmentalists view these nativars as the path to the future of habitat restoration, while others see them as simply another foolish attempt at human domination over nature. In practice, it may be a bit of both.

Besides changing plant bloom and foliage to an unhealthy degree, many cultivars currently on the market are also weaker to environmental stressors than their unchanged counterparts. This is because current horticultural trends rely on cloning in order to propagate desirable qualities once they are found. This practice can lead to those new plants having less genetic diversity between themselves. Less genetic diversity means that it is easier for a pest or disease to take advantage of a shared weakness in the species. There are varieties being bred to become more resistant to pests and diseases as well, however, so some of these weaknesses may soon be mitigated. Many growers and scientists feel that these downsides are small prices to pay for the benefits that specialized plants could offer. While on the surface this raises red flags of unwarranted human interference, here the fallibility of human science can perhaps be a bonus, as our clumsy tinkerings may have as much chance to propagate subtle changes quickly reversed by natural selection as they do to cause lasting damage. The impact of cultivars as a whole on wildlife is a hot topic in current research, however there are still a good deal of unknowns. Until more research is done on the true effects of these altered plants on our environment, staying away from any cultivars that change a plant's flowers, leaves, or overall shape to a large degree is a smart move. If you want to play it extra safe, your local nursery should be able to point you in the direction of their unchanged, or straight, native species. New cultivars are constantly being developed in the pursuit of restoring natural habitat, and there have already been some incredible success stories regarding the use of specific man-made plant varieties.

Over the last few hundred years, the landscapes of America have changed drastically due to foreign invaders. Pests and diseases from abroad are constantly being tossed upon our shores, brought to a new land filled with plentiful food and more importantly devoid of their natural predators. This has led to huge swaths of destruction due to the corresponding unchecked population growths of these organisms. The vast majority of the elms and chestnuts that once dominated American temperate forests were wiped out as diseases attacked their defenseless innards throughout the 1900s. Many of the ash trees in the northeast states are currently under attack from the relentless assaults of the introduced emerald ash borer. The spotted lanternfly, an introduced sap-sucking insect, has begun decimating trees and vines alike since arriving here in 2014. These are just a few examples of many, and in most cases the first treatment used to combat such attacks is heavy pesticide use. Unfortunately, many of these pesticides have unknown long-term effects on plants and animals. Exciting developments in cultivars of both elms and chestnuts are rearing new generations that appear to be resistant to the diseases that almost made them extinct. These same cultivars have shown to have little to no negative impacts on surrounding wildlife as well. With luck, similar varieties can be developed to become resistant to other such dangers. If these varieties turn out to be more resistant to stressors while having minimal impact on their environments, they could reduce the amount of pesticides used to combat invasive threats. In such a situation, cultivars are sometimes the lesser of two evils, as even their impacts on the lives around them seem to pale in comparison to the lasting legacy of even a single pesticide application.

Due to the rapid proliferation of urban developments, large scale agriculture based on huge swaths of single crops, and the 'spray and forget' mindset surrounding many pesticides, humans have become a scourge upon the earth. Many environmentalists are quick to point out that the rapid pace of extinctions due to human intervention is a travesty the likes of which the world has never seen. This is not exactly true. The earth has been privy to such mass death before—in the form of meteorite impact. It is now scientifically accepted that around 65 million years ago a large meteorite made contact with Mexico, blasting enough superheated particulates into the air that half of the world's sunlight was blocked out for at least 10 years.

This and other equally impactful side effects of such a collision are thought to have led to the extinction of around 75% the species around at that time. While there have been multiple mass extinctions throughout the history of our planet, this extraterrestrial impact is thought to have caused the most rapid loss of life. Unfortunately for the plant and animal species alive today, it seems that the current rate of extinctions occurring around us is approaching meteoric speeds. It is of critical importance that humans as a species pull our heads from our collective rears and begin to take real steps towards slowing this decline.

As we begin to search the universe for answers to how and why Earth has become a wellspring of life, it is becoming clear that living beings are some of the rarest things in existence. From a purely selfish standpoint, the lessons to be learned from the myriad of lives being played out around us are endless. Consider the impacts on travel if we were to unlock the mysteries behind the incredibly efficient flight systems of insects, or the advancements in storage technology if the meticulous secrets of pollen construction were revealed. The plants and animals around us are more than just scenery, they are the rarest and most valuable resources we could ever hope to come into contact with. As inhabitants of the modern world, it is our responsibility to ensure that these resources are never lost through our actions. By maintaining an iron-clad vigilance over how you impact the natural world around you, it is possible to make a real and lasting positive change. Re-establishing native wildlife habitat is one of the most important and surprisingly easy things you can do in and around your property. Leave areas 'wild' wherever possible, and encourage anyone who you see spraying pesticides to consider whether such applications make the most long term ecological sense. With the appropriate amount of care and forethought, human intervention in the natural world does not have to be all bad. In fact, it seems to be exactly what our planet needs.

Thank you for reading.

The next installment of *A Guide to the Wonderful World Around Us* will be coming soon!

Please follow along at sprigglys.com or on social media @sprigglys_beescaping.

If you would like to see our list of favorite resources or want to know the name of an artist featured in this book, please contact us at info@sprigglys.com.

BLMT
6.19 L

Black Mountain Public Library
105 Dougherty St.
Black Mountain, NC 28711

Made in the USA
Columbia, SC
06 May 2019